Praises for *Truth In The Rivers*

"This inspiring book reminds me of why I love what I do. Watching a child's senses spark while nature's gifts are surrounding and inviting them into a world of sharing, caring, and understanding is priceless. We should all take a lesson from this book, and nature, by slowing down, listening, being patient and never letting the fire of a child's imagination and love for learning burn out."

—Jody Moats, Naturalist, South Dakota Game, Fish & Parks

"*Truth In The Rivers* is an unforgettable journey for the reader with indelible moments of truth and understanding of what it is to be human. From 'Ganbare'—the story of a Japanese American family interned during World War II, depicted in a series of remarkable water colors by Howard Horii—to 'An Underlying Set of Truths' where we are confronted with painful and brutal reminders of the Civil Rights Movement of the 1960s. These are powerful stories drawn from raw, unfiltered life experience and beautifully articulated by Bruce Hopkins."

—Gretchen Gondek, General Manager, KWIT-KOJI FM90 Public Radio

"Bruce Hopkins addresses issues that are of great importance and concern in our communal life...civil rights, the environment, our children. He does this through prose, poetry, paintings, and personal stories. His philosophy of life and his observations about life are both informative and enlightening. I was personally interested in reading about the Japanese American internment during the Second World War. At that time I had a brief correspondence with a girl my age (9 years old) who had been interned with her family at a place called Poston, Arizona. Our Methodist Church in my small Iowa hometown had sent a care package to the residents of Poston. Soon after that I received a letter and photo from the young girl. I have often wondered what became of her and her family after the war was over."

—Joy Corning, Iowa Lt. Governor (1990-1998)

"Bruce Hopkins draws deeply from his extensive work as an environmentalist, educator, and writer to craft an elegant literary song addressing thoughtful introspections of Japanese American internment, 1960s Civil Rights, and preparing our children for an environmentally rewarding future. Sung in perfect three-part harmony, this work will resonate with the reader long after the final note is delivered. These seemingly diverse topics, under Hopkins' deft creative conjuring, effectively and aesthetically blend these into a gratifying sensory symphony."

—John Busbee, The Culture Buzz, Des Moines, Iowa

"Bruce Hopkins weaves together seemingly disparate strands: Howard N. Horii's graceful watercolor paintings of scenes from his family's time in an Arizona internment camp during World War II; with essays about the Civil Rights Movement of the 1960s; together with poems, essays, paintings, and photographs touting the lessons of nature and nature forays with children. The result? An artful tapestry that reveals how deeply nature, culture, politics, and education entwine to impact us all."

—Cheryl Fusco Johnson; Author, and Host of Writers' Voices KRUU

"In this one short volume, Bruce Hopkins has applied three distinct forms: prose, poetry, and painting, to three different subjects to show that our experiences have a profound influence on us. He encourages us to use our relationships with family and friends to enhance their lives and, by doing so, help them make a better world for all. He has reaffirmed a major motivation for my Peace Corps service many years ago, that we are all connected."

—Jack Fitzpatrick, Architect and Peace Corps Volunteer (1970-1972)

"Heartbreaking and heartwarming stories about how strong we are in the face of war and unjust internments and how much we love places we call Home, and above all our Children. Remembering post WWII in Poland and living in America since 1981, I want to thank you Bruce Hopkins and Howard Horii for this beautiful book."

—Ewa Nogiec, Provincetown Artist

"The Horii family story is so inspiring, a test of the human spirit and how adversity can be overcome, made into positive actions during those years in the camp and turned into successes throughout each of their lives. Howard's watercolor images are so powerful and the feeling of the moment captured is so strong, whether depicting the serenity of the desert or the chaos at the Santa Anita racetrack, the paintings are so moving. This is a fantastic journey to read and to experience through the artwork!"

—Suzan Lucas Santiago, Principal, SANTIAGO design group llc

"These lovely essays, poems, and paintings hold important lessons to share with the children in our lives: respect for the beauty of nature, celebration of art and creativity, justice and fairness as basic rights for all people, as well as the importance of building deep connections to the people we love, the communities that nurture us, and the heritage that shapes us."

—Deborah Stahl, Early Childhood Education Consultant, Winner of the 2013 Work Life Legacy Award

"Howard Horii's haunting images create an understanding of how goodness and beauty can outlive injustice, and sets the tone for this important book, which at its heart is about generational activism."

—Lydia Whitefield, Environmental and Civil Rights Activist

5.30.14

To Joanne and Larry

With fondness and good wishes

Truth In The Rivers

Photo by Ken Horii

Howard N. Horii (left) and Bruce Hopkins

Bruce Hopkins

Watercolors by Howard N. Horii

Howard N. Horii

Ice Cube Press LLC

North Liberty, Iowa

Truth in the Rivers

ISBN 9781888160727 1 3 5 7 9 8 6 4 2

Library of Congress Preassigned Number: 2013936190

Ice Cube Press, LLC (Est. 1993)
205 N. Front Street
North Liberty, Iowa 52317
w: www.icecubepress.com
e: steve@icecubepress.com
twitter: @icecubepress

The paper used in this publication meets the minimum requirements of the American National Standard for Information Sciences—Permanence of Paper for Printed Library Materials, ANSI Z39.48-1992.

Manufactured in the United States of America with recycled paper.

Watercolors by Howard N. Horii are from his own collection and from the collections of:
The family of Helen and Jack Okano
Louise and George Kawamoto
Mary and Kazuo Kajiyama
The family of George and Nancy Horii
The family of Jim and Jeanette Horii
Harry and Chita Horii
Robert and Mary Horii
Dr. Steve Horii and Gail Fishman
Ken Horii and Harriet Pappas
Jane and Bob Clancy

Dedication:
Howard and Paula Horii

Special Acknowledgements to:
Jeanette Hopkins
Milton Harrison
Louise "Lou" Porter
Steve Semken
My four daughters and eleven grandchildren,
whose sense of fairness and justice sustains me.

Marc Embree and Jane Bunnell for their research at the Japanese American National Museum in Los Angeles.

Ken Horii and Harriet Pappas for their assistance with the images in the book.

Contents

Introduction

My whole philosophy—which is very real—teaches acquiescence and optimism. Only when I see how much work is to be done, what room for a poet—for any spiritualist—in this great, intelligent, sensual, and avaricious America, I lament my fumbling fingers and stammering tongue.

—Ralph Waldo Emerson[1]

This small missive is not without purpose or contention. My wife and children's book author, Jeanette Hopkins, and I work from what we term a sense of place perspective. We believe that children should be afforded every opportunity to learn in a natural way, to become familiar with the common names of flora and fauna in regional areas, to have shared the stories of their elders, and to know themselves as part of a larger community. We have places we hold reverentially close where we go to walk about, partake of good food and conversation, rummage through old books, and reconnect with history, architecture, and neighborhood.

We concern ourselves with making a better future for our children by working in schools and communities on issues relating to literacy. Every child of every age and circumstance deserves to be touched by stories—those of imagination, of heroic dimension, and of history. Often rural people, who live with generational history, know community as a living and vibrant entity, where old gravestones

1 *The Correspondence of Thomas Carlyle and RW Emerson*, 1834-1872, Vol. 1 LXVII. Emerson to Carlyle. Ralph Waldo Emerson (1803-1882) American essayist, philosopher, and poet.

speak, where family lines bend and converge, creating connections and continuity. In this political culture, the purpose of schooling is often defined in terms of employability. Education emerges as a skill set designed to improve student proficiency in high stake tests. Education becomes that which can be measured, to the detriment of learning. Equally important are literature and art, the world of the imagination, and a deep appreciation for the immensely different ways in which people live in community. Ashley Montagu[2] was referring to this when he spoke of the human need for participation in a caring environment as well as for spiritual and physical contact. We all have an innate need to live in intimate proximity to that which sustains and nurtures us.

The overall tenet of these essays and poems is that our perspective on the character of a place is a reflection of the qualities held so dear by society. Woven into the fabric of these stories is the struggle for civil rights, for African American citizens, for Japanese American citizens, in essence for *all* citizens. These brief scenarios are derived from my personal experiences as a young teacher in Nebraska, New York, Iowa, and the deep South. As a teacher I have always believed that whatever happens to the least of us, happens to *all* of us. Democracy is the most demanding form of government. At different points in our history only landowners could vote, Native Americans had no rights, African Americans were enslaved, and women did not have the right to vote. Our past continues to haunt the present as we hear some church leaders speak of knowing "what is right" to justify their opposition to gay marriage. Social change does not come easily, and inflexible belief systems often detract from change occurring. Leading up to and following the 2012 Presidential election, we have seen major movement on several key social issues such as the status of gays in the military, women in combat, a more inclusive approach to immigration reform, and a far-ranging discussion on the Second Amendment.

I am deeply honored that my brother-in-law, artist, and architect Howard Nobuo Horii, agreed to provide watercolors for this book and to have shared a perspective of one Japanese American's experience of having been evacuated and put in an internment camp during World War II, following the bombing of Pearl

2 Ashley Montagu (1905-1999) British American anthropologist and humanist.

Harbor. The existence of internment camps throughout the United States during the war led the way to our exploration of Howard's experiences as a student, a teacher, a farm laborer, an architect, and an artist. We were struck by the fact that although there were Japanese internment camps and German and Italian POW camps located at that time throughout the areas where we had lived and worked, we were unaware of the full extent of this part of our history, causing me to recommit myself to a more accurate portrayal of the American experience.

I am equally honored to be able to share the memories and experiences of my friends Louise ("Lou") Porter, Milton Harrison, and my teaching colleagues in Grand Island, Nebraska, from the 1960s, that tumultuous time in our history when the civil rights movement took center stage and brought about significant changes that moved our country's attitudes more closely in the direction of fairness and justice. As this book took form, I became more focused on how personal qualities speak to individual accomplishments. Included in the qualities that Howard, Lou, and Milton have in common are perseverance in the face of daunting odds and an indomitable spirit that carries one forward, all the while optimistically encouraging others to do the same. For me, they sustain the faith we have in the difference that people of good will can make in the lives of children and in the broader community. *Truth in the Rivers* is sustained by the assumption that moral courage drives democratic government and that at times we need the guidance of thoughtful, informed, and just people to set its compass right.

In this book I have attempted to encapsulate in essays, poems, and through Howard's artwork, a glimpse of how the issues of nature, of culture, of politics and of education impact *all* of society. Thomas Jefferson[3] spoke of how an educated electorate is necessary for democratic government and this need still rings true today. Thurgood Marshall's[4] reaction to the lynchings during the worst of our unjust racial times was recently shared in national newspapers. I was reminded of how the photos of such terrible violence against humanity have impacted my own life, and strengthened my resolve against injustice of any kind. Justice Marshall remembered the smiles on the faces of the spectators as they viewed these awful

3 Thomas Jefferson (1743-1826) Third President of the United States.

4 Thurgood Marshall (1908-1993) United States Supreme Court Justice. He was the Court's 96th justice and its first African American justice.

acts of human degradation. That young children were present during these most inhumane experiences, ensuring the continuity of such behavior, bothered him the most.

We must all recognize the civic and moral responsibility that we have to our children. While reading this collection I hope you will find some of the calm that William Cullen Bryant[5] found on entering the woods. I hope you will also find a sense of community as the interplay of the natural environments, social settings, and cultural experiences we all share are portrayed. I hope, most of all, that our younger generations come to know the deep affection in which they deserve to be held, and a future consistent with our most profound democratic values.

Selecting *Truth in the Rivers* as the title for this book, I was struck by the connection between the rivers of Iowa and rivers everywhere, specifically the character of place, and the health of communities. It's difficult to imagine Nebraska without the Platte River and the migratory route of the sandhill cranes. The same holds true to the DeSoto National Wildlife Refuge in Iowa bordering the Missouri River, where hundreds of thousands of snow geese descend from slate grey skies each fall. The rivers, the oceans, and the lakes and their viscosity in human and other species migrations assist in connecting us all to a broader understanding of community.

5 William Cullen Bryant (1794-1878) American poet and editor.

Photo by George Kawamoto

Howard N. Horii as a young man sketching in northern Michigan while visiting his sister Louise and her husband George Kawamoto who settled in Detroit after the war where they established a successful portrait and commercial photography studio.

A Society of Children

I drove to the elementary school,
careful to arrive before
the press of parents
and grandparents…

It is December,
cold winds sweep down,
over the parking lot…
cooling the roadway
between where I am parked
and the green dumpster
where I wait.

Children rush past me,
chatting incessantly,
laughing,
more tumbling
than running.

My grandchildren
have adapted my attitude
towards orderliness…
arriving disheveled.

After most of the others have departed,
the lady,
who holds the stop sign erect,
while crossing the busy street
escorting children…
and parents,
has left.

The pack breaks
as one of the youngest
sprints towards the car to claim rights…

calling, "Shotgun"...
jumping into the front seat.

With us,
a neighbor girl,
a fixture in this little band...
the clarifier of rumors,
the "knower" of truth...
A prized status, able to transcend any argument.

As the children empty from the car,
I tell each that I love him or her...
Always,
the last wisp of a girl,
echoes back...
the words I had just spoken.

The Gathering

In late fall,
    Garter snakes
    gather in large balls.

On cold winter nights
    white tail deer gather
    in extensive herds

Ashley Montagu
    may have given credence
    to the art of touching,

Old Hippies
    lived by it.

Voices From the Cliffs

No one taught me
about the
wisdom imparted
when words shouted
at the cliffs
returned in kind.

Cliffs are best
studied in isolation
the eyes drawn
ever upward...
held in place,
by awe and
wonder.

The oldest trees
I've ever encountered,
grow on such cliffs...
gnarled, ancient
conifers
are at home
in the desert heat
or the fierce winds
of winter

I'm ever grateful
these ancient crusty rocks
make for me
death palatable.

Betrayal

Often we are betrayed
by what we've learned.

The mind does not
always catalogue
outside the lines,
where every new
experience happens.

Ganbare

Ganbare
The Artist's Palette
The Art of Making Do

Butte Camp (Camp 2) at the Gila River Relocation Center in Arizona.

Ganbare

Morita, the kid from Camp 2, would finally hit the peak of the mountain he chose to climb before he learned to walk. He would only hope to pass this small example of persistence of continued effort on to those who receive no encouragement for dreaming their dreams and hope only to hope beyond their means; that they might live and breathe long enough to fulfill both....[6]

—Pat Morita[7]

Prior to the United States entrance into World War II, the country was aware that we were involved in the fighting in Europe against the Nazis. Our pilots were active in France (before France fell to Germany), and later in Great Britain. In spite of the growing specter of the United States being pulled into the war, Japan's surprise attack on Pearl Harbor on December 7, 1941, was felt with such magnitude that a Declaration of War quickly followed.

People in the United States had been quite aware of the cat and mouse games going on in the Atlantic between German U-boats and American submarines. German and American subs had exchanged torpedoes and one American sub, the

6 From the 50-year Commemorative Booklet (1995), *Gila River Relocation Center, 1942-1945*, Noriyuki (Pat) Morita.

7 Noriyuki (Pat) Morita (1932-2005) Japanese American actor known for *Happy Days* and *The Karate Kid* (for which he earned an Academy Award nomination for best supporting actor). He was 11 years old when he was moved from a sanitarium near Sacramento (where he had been recovering from spinal tuberculosis since the age of two) to join his parents in the internment camp in Arizona. Morita and his family were in the same camp as Howard Horii's family, Butte Camp (Camp 2).

Reuben James, was sunk in the North Atlantic. Yet we were accustomed to viewing ourselves apart from the rest of the world, even with a strident voice of isolationism. The nation that declared war on Japan was a, "fifth-rate military power," whose, "staggering losses at Pearl Harbor," included, "eight battleships sunk or badly damaged," and, "hundreds of planes destroyed." For the Allies, the news early in the war as America became involved was catastrophic, with "one crushing Allied defeat after another… For Americans, the shock of losing much of the U.S. fleet at Pearl Harbor was followed by Japanese conquests of Guam, Wake Island, and the Philippines."[8]

News of the Pearl Harbor attack shocked the nation, but perhaps nowhere more so than in California. A recent discussion that I had with a Navy veteran who was stationed in California at the time was of the anti-aircraft guns firing into the night sky, and the talk of a pending invasion. It was against this backdrop that Japanese Americans found themselves caught up in the national hysteria of war.

The broad range of human emotions only hints at the complexity of feelings when they learned of Executive Order 9066 signed by President Franklin D. Roosevelt on February 19, 1942. The order authorized tens of thousands of American citizens of Japanese ancestry and resident aliens from Japan to be detained and relocated from their homes.

For the family of Howard Nobuo Horii, this news came in the form of a legal notice affixed to telephone poles throughout their community in Redondo Beach, California. Their property consisted of a barn, three small houses that his father had built himself, and a horse, all of which were hurriedly sold for a meager sum. Because Howard's parents were first generation Japanese American (Issei), they could not become American citizens or own land.[9]

Like shattered glass, Howard and his family found themselves abruptly separated from the community they had lived in and known so well, adrift in the most volatile of circumstances, but any fear was overridden by the realization that the

8 From *Citizens of London* by Lynne Olson, Random House (2010).

9 Their children, however, the *Nisei* (second generation), could become US citizens, as the fourteenth amendment to the Constitution allows that anyone born on United States soil is automatically a United States citizen. In 1913, California passed the Alien Land Law, which denied "all aliens ineligible for citizenship," which included Japanese immigrants, the right to own land in the state. From *World War II Chronicles,* a quarterly newsletter of the World War II Veterans Committee, Issue XXII, Autumn, 2003.

only realities to be protected were family remembrances and those shared ideas of the spirit so critical to their survival. Something as simple as the family photograph they saved, taken just a year earlier, of Howard's parents, his seven brothers and sisters and his brother-in-law reflects an inherent respect for personal dignity, and social decorum.

I find myself sensing the isolation of these Japanese Americans as they came to grips with the emotionalism driving the President's executive order[10] and the reality of having to survive the immediate future. Family elders settled on the paramount need to keep the family together. Initially, for a period of about six months, Howard and his family were sent to an assembly center at Santa Anita Racetrack in California where Howard sketched a riot that had broken out that he later made into a watercolor. There were no accommodations for sleeping at the racetrack other than dirty horse stalls and mattresses made of straw. Even in the eyes of Howard's stoicism he remembers this period as the most difficult of times. While there, a friend of Howard's younger brother, Harry, visited the family to bring word that the poster Harry had earlier entered in their junior high school contest in support of the war effort had won a prize. His friend, who was not Japanese, accompanied by his parents who had found out where the Horii family had been relocated, wanted Harry to know the good news, and to personally give him the prize that he had won—a war bond.

From Santa Anita, the family was relocated to the Gila River Relocation Center in Arizona, located on the Gila River Indian Reservation about 50 miles southeast of Phoenix, near the town of Rivers. There were two camps on the site, Canal Camp, and the larger Butte Camp (Camp 2), where the Horii family lived, along with about 13,000 other internees, in small rooms and crowded barracks. For three years, Butte Camp became their home, and Howard's canvas. He sketched the barracks, the water tower and flowering cactus while there. Despite their hardships, Howard recalls the beauty of the desert and the resourcefulness and resilience of his fellow internees, many of whom were farmers, as they became self-sufficient by turning dry

10 There were many close to the President opposed to the order, including his wife, Eleanor, who in 1943 visited the internment camp where Howard's family was relocated, Butte Camp at the Gila River Relocation Center in Arizona. Howard recalls being encouraged by the First Lady's visit. Decades later, Congress passed and President Ronald Reagan signed legislation, titled the Civil Liberties Act of 1988, which apologized for the internment on behalf of the U.S. government.

canals into rivers using water from flash floods and the dams built earlier by Native Americans, and growing enough food for themselves and other camps.

What these detainees and their overseers had in common was the experience of a world turned upside down. The fabric of culture that sustained predictability in the defining of roles, social decorum, expectations, and dignity was left tattered and torn. Those imbued with authority, guards and other people employed to work in these new assembly and relocation centers, most likely had little previous contact with Japanese Americans and in the worst of scenarios felt threatened by cultural demeanors that were unfamiliar to them. The detainees, most of whom were accustomed to a tight culture with predictive qualities defined by family, religion and antiquity, found their lives defined and controlled by a set of circumstances where the rules of the game were in flux and they were treated as a threat to the nation they had revered. Pat Morita would later write that he remembered attending his first school class in the relocation camp in Arizona and later recalled the irony and poignancy of reciting the Pledge of Allegiance "while noting in his young mind's eye barbed wire and manned guard towers."[11]

The remarkable resilience and strength exhibited by Howard and his family during this time was reinforced by all of their many accomplishments and successes later in life. There's a Japanese word for courage, determination, and resilience—the word is *ganbare*. The injustice of internment foisted on a people who above all saw themselves as American confronted the Japanese Americans with a host of questions, but whatever sense of injustice that occurred morphed into a determination, once the war was over, to quickly move on with a spirit of perseverance and purpose, ganbare again.

11 From the 50-year Commemorative Booklet (1995), *Gila River Relocation Center, 1942-1945*.

The Horii family photograph taken in 1940 in front of their home on Pacific Avenue in Redondo Beach, California, where they had a small farm and grocery store. Standing, from left: Mary Kiyoko, Louise Aiko, Helen Misuye, Jack Yasuo Okano (Helen's husband), George Fusao, Howard Nobuo, Jim Yoshio, Harry Itsuo, and Robert Sachio. Seated, their parents, from left: Konobu and Rikimatsu.

Our Visitor ..

· OUR FIRST LADY ·

Eleanor Roosevelt visiting the internment camp in 1943. From a page in the 1943 school yearbook that was produced at the camp (Butte High School, Rivers, Arizona, War Relocation Authority, Gila Center).

In the middle of the desert, with mountains looming in the distance, the barracks at Butte Camp located on the Gila River Indian Reservation in Arizona, where the Horii family and some 13,000 others were interned for three years, from 1942 to 1945.

The Monument

I can hardly imagine
the images in
Howard Horii's mind
as he painstakingly
painted the names
of Japanese American soldiers

...first interned as prisoners
in their own land
then allowed into the
armed forces,

on the Gila River memorial monument
in Arizona.

The internment process,
the denial of citizenship
had foisted upon him

an acute awareness
of his Asian heritage
and identity as an American...

in a montage of conflictive
images.

Now there was,
at least,

recognition for those
who had served...

and confirmation
of his sacred self

and his art.

The Artist's Palette

It's not what you look at that matters,
it's what you see.
—Henry David Thoreau[12]

Fate intervened in Howard Nobuo Horii's life, yanking him from his teenage years into adulthood as the impact of the bombing of Pearl Harbor[13] was brought home to California. Within weeks Howard's life was transformed: from an honor student in Redondo Union High School, to the education afforded him as a scholarship student at the Otis Art Institute in Los Angeles, to the assembly center at Santa Anita Racetrack, then to the internment camp in Arizona. Much was lost, home, the promise of a good education in art, his family's personal property and thriving business, as they were forcibly relocated to new and unfamiliar surroundings.

California would totally encapsulate Howard's early days. His friendships involved swimming in the Pacific Ocean, working alongside his family, and salvaging whatever nature and the scraps from the local lumberyard offered up … to build tire swings, forts, and all kinds of contraptions with his friends and his brother George, that tilted Howard's eye in the direction of architecture that ultimately, along with his art, became his life's work.

12 Henry David Thoreau (1817-1862) American writer, philosopher, and naturalist.

13 The next day, on December 8, 1941, Congress declared war on Japan and a few days later, on December 11, Congress declared war on Germany.

Following Japan's decision to attack Pearl Harbor, circumstances changed the life of every Japanese American, past, present, and future. The memories for Howard's family were made even more cogent as their destiny was, for the most part, outside of their control. His family's grocery store and small truck farm in Redondo Beach, the crops so self-sustaining, so meticulously cared for, would not be theirs to keep. His father's genius in building three separate homes, each better able to withstand the force of a California earthquake would become prideful memories. Also shattered were the community of close friends and acquaintances whose activities gained meaning through shared holidays and social gatherings such as on New Year's Day when they celebrated the holiday *Oshogatsu,* a time of socializing, feasting, and fellowship that involved the custom of *mochitsuki,* the pounding of mochi or rice cakes. Howard recalls that the day you were offered to use a giant wooden mallet to do the pounding was a milestone in one's life. As a young boy, he was particularly in awe of the turners of the rice, who always seemed so courageous to him because of their willingness and ability to quickly put their hands into the large wooden tub and turn the rice before the next pound. There was a rhythm to the pounding and the turning that was soothing and reassuring to his young eyes and ears.

Just prior to the war, the eighteen-year-old Howard had been offered a scholarship to the Otis Art Institute in Los Angeles, which he was attending when the news came of the attack on Pearl Harbor, changing not only his life but his art. As he and his family were relocated to the assembly center at Santa Anita Racetrack and then to the internment camp in Arizona, his paintings gained vibrancy and intensity as he sketched, painted and utilized watercolors to record what he experienced and what he saw. The riot at the Santa Anita Racetrack, the barracks, and the water tower at the internment camp, and the desolation and the beauty of the Arizona desert were all captured first on paper and then on canvas by his ever observant eyes and recorded for posterity by the artistry of his hand and his brush. One of the unique attributes of Howard's paintings was in having the constructions and landscapes speak for themselves. A notable exception was in painting the riot at Santa Anita Racetrack where the paradox of social decision making blurred the natural attributes of the setting. Howard's painting of the riot at the racetrack pulls us into a violent setting where the deep oranges and reds speak to the out of control nature of the fire and the portrayal of the human element is one embossed by violence and a loss of connectivity. Later, at the internment camp in Arizona, Howard found serenity in the yellow flowers of the cactus and the inherent beauty of the landscape, while the water tower and barracks are portrayed in stark, lifeless, drab grays and browns. Seldom do we find people in Howard's paintings. In the Santa Anita painting, they are there as elements being acted upon. Later in his works, the landscapes or cityscapes make their own statements about the human condition. As an architectural student at Pratt Institute in Brooklyn in the 1950s he developed a perspective on the design of prisons in his senior thesis which assumed many of the human qualities he became concerned with while in the internment camp.

During the time his family was in the internment camp the country was experiencing a serious labor shortage, particularly in the agricultural industry, due to all the manpower and womanpower[14] being devoted to fighting the war abroad and working in the war industries at home. The country needed farm workers. In late summer 1943, Howard, his brother George, and their father volunteered and were allowed to go from the internment camp in Arizona to Ault, Colorado, to work as sharecroppers, joining his older sister Helen and her husband Jack Okano and their young daughter Tachi who had gone earlier. They worked for several months before returning to the camp on a farm owned by German Americans, working alongside German soldiers from nearby POW camps. They grew cucumbers and potatoes, sometimes picking several tons of cucumbers a day. Because George had been driving since he was twelve years old, he would drive the farm owner's truck fifty miles away to deliver the cucumbers to a plant where they were processed to feed the army. Two years later, in 1945, George was inducted into the U.S. Army himself and served in the occupation forces in Germany where he became a driver for the commanding officers.

14 American women entered the workforce in unprecedented numbers during World War II, as widespread male enlistment left gaping holes in the industrial labor force. "Rosie the Riveter," star of a government campaign aimed at recruiting female workers for the munitions industry, became perhaps the most iconic image of working women during the war. From www.history.com/topics/rosie-the-riveter.

One of the most compelling aspects of Howard's and his family's internment was how they intuitively adapted their knowledge and inventiveness as farmers to their wartime experiences.

They took on the task of raising vegetables in Colorado with the same focus and intensity of purpose as they did in the internment camp in Arizona and on their small truck farm in California. They demonstrated very quickly that they were experienced farmers and could bring about the most effective and efficient results if they were allowed to follow the agricultural practices and methodologies they knew best. They also felt it was the patriotic thing to do, to farm and grow vegetables for the troops and others, always deeply motivated by a respect for the land and the environment.

In Colorado, Howard's paintings gained vibrancy as he sketched, painted, and utilized watercolors to record the intense beauty that he saw. He continued to hone his ability to find the unique essence of place even as his life's journey took him back to Arizona from Colorado, and then after the war, to New York City, where buildings and bridges now emerged from his artist's palette, inspiring him to study architecture as a natural and logical extension of his art. The intonations of Howard's work as an artist, and later as an architect, constantly involved his ability to be pulled into a setting and find the face of that place.

Howard's approach to many of his life's complexities was one of a powerful observer seldom crossing the line as a political advocate. His experiences in the internment camps allowed him an opportunity to teach art classes at Butte High School by receiving teacher training from on-site instructors who came in from Arizona State College. When he moved to New York City after the war to study art and architecture, and after receiving his architectural degree from Pratt Institute and practicing architecture, he utilized those teaching skills by teaching evenings in the construction management program at Pratt for 44 years. For several summers he conducted a walking tour of New York City that he created for Pratt students, giving lectures about the city's famous buildings and the architects who designed them. When Howard speaks of buildings or of nature, interpreting the shape and fabric of the world around him, he is the practicing artist without the brush motivated not by politics but by what he observes.

One of Howard's most memorable expressions as an artist occurred when he was in the internment camp, and he had painted the names of Japanese American soldiers from the Gila River Relocation Center who served their country onto a memorial monument located on a hill overlooking the camp. The monument was built of concrete with wood panels where Howard had meticulously painted the soldiers' names. Decades later, when the opportunity arose for Howard to revisit the camp, he saw that the concrete structure was still standing, but the wood panels and names were gone. Gone too were the water tower and the barracks that he had sketched and painted for posterity. Only the foundations, bringing to mind a sense of loss, yet hope for the future, remained.

The riot at Santa Anita Racetrack.

Howard contrasts the starkness of the internal landscape with the beauty of the external landscape by depicting a drab sky over the internment camp barracks and water tower, and a breathtaking sunset in the desert.

Farm scenes painted by Howard during the months spent in Colorado with his father and brother at a critical time during the war when the country needed farm workers.

Fascinated by the waterways of New York City, Howard drew inspiration from the Brooklyn Bridge (top) which spans the East River and the High Bridge Water Tower which overlooks the Harlem River.

Howard recognized that whether stored in a tower on top of a hill in Arizona or in towers on the roofs of high buildings in New York, water is critical to bringing the streams of life to the desert and the city.

Photo by Howard Horii

Photo by Paula Horii

Howard revisited Butte Camp in 1979 finding the wood panels missing from the Gila River memorial monument but the concrete structure still standing.

In Character

Walking

on an isolated

Midwestern bike trail

Cottonwood leaves

adorned the overpass

there is a perfection

in the early form

of discarded cottonwood leaves.

Later, they will grow in character

tattered and torn

and imbued

with their own particular

loveliness.

Transformation

Mountains are
        never still
it's just not
        their nature.

Large moss encrusted
        boulders host the
        very trees
                that will split
        them as severely
as a killer frost.

Tsunamis
        begin in splendid
        isolation, as a fissure
                in the earth sends
                one tectonic plate
        upward over the face
                of another
        the uplifted water
                forms a wave
                which only blasts
                        into being, as it
        approaches land.

The Art of Making Do

But yield who will to their separation,
My object in living is to unite
My avocation and my vocation
As my two eyes make one in sight.
Only where love and need are one,
And the work is play for mortal stakes,
Is the deed ever really done
For Heaven and the future's sakes.
—Robert Frost[15]

Internationally, following the Great Depression, World War II was imminent, but locally, for Howard Nobuo Horii as a young boy there were only opportunities and adventure. Growing up near a neighborhood lumberyard work and play were one, providing endless materials and found objects for crafting and building, for "making do." Salvaging lumber was not work, it was more an artistic endeavor. The endeavor might have, or might not have, any particular purpose in mind. Once, when Howard and his older brother George and their friends had amassed a particularly notable stack of lumber,

15 Robert Frost (1874-1963) American poet. From his poem "Two Tramps in Mud Time."

the bountiful attributes of Mother Nature led to an inescapable conclusion. They just had to build a raft. Their craft emerged from the dimensions of the available pieces of wood. Fitting the pieces together resembled the challenge of assembling piles of small puzzle pieces absent the picture of the puzzle itself. These were times when work, play, toys, and tools were inherently connected.

Visiting with Howard, he speaks almost reverently of a surfboard that he and George constructed in the workshop they built together with their father. The finished product was twelve feet long and made of redwood (the ends and sides) and marine plywood (the top). They constructed it over Christmas, and successfully field-tested it in the Pacific Ocean at Redondo Beach in California on New Year's Eve. He tells of many excursions for found objects, some involving expeditions to the city dump, a veritable gold mine for youngsters looking for discarded treasures. One such trip resulted in the salvaging of a pair of roller skates, the foundation for the most memorable of racing carts.

Whether a surfboard, racing cart, or a raft, the task of finding the perfect piece of wood, sorting it, deciding how to lash, nail, and put pieces together, was decidedly different from working in a production facility or an assembly line. The objective for each moment might be to simply salvage wood. Opportunity presented itself as twine was scattered about the work space. Work assignments for Howard and his brother and friends emerged in an equally strange and mysterious way. If a handsaw was needed to cut the wood to length, whoever could most easily lay hands on a cross cut saw would undertake the problem. Boredom was seldom a part of their day. They swam in the ocean, swung on an old tire attached to a cable strung over the salt lake, and played basketball shooting a rag-filled football into a hoop they had ingeniously constructed from the bamboo rim of a big barrel of soy sauce.

The Great Depression conditioned this generation with the necessity of thrift and hard work. The opportunity to barter a few coins for fresh fish afforded itself nearly every day. Howard's father knew people at the Redondo Beach pier and would send his boys to buy fish. They would come back with a big bunch of mackerel for which they paid the princely sum of 25 cents. They also bought smelt, and with their father, built a high tower from salvaged lumber, using a rope and pulley to hoist it up on a fishing net that Howard and George had found washed up on the beach, so that the smelt could dry high above the ground, protected from insects and small animals. Howard's father liked to cook and did most of the cooking for the family, using fresh vegetables from the family farm and fresh fish from the pier.

In Howard's childhood, one of the most interesting social attributes was that one could simply be promoted in the eyes of others if he lived next to a lumber yard. If he could lay his hands on a saw...if an older brother owned a wagon, then he could take the lead in terms of helping others to solve a building problem. Take the case of finding a treasure trove of used lumber filled with nails: the lumber was cleaned, the nails straightened to a familiar form, and in good time, latches or hinges were found to build the perfect craft.

The process was further enriched by the notable absence in that day of hardware stores, or the large construction megastores of today. Encouraged by their parents and their brothers and sisters, the challenge of "making do" with found objects for Howard and George was the norm. The integration of their childhood endeavors and work was common, where work was play and play was work, so much so that later in their lives would have practical applications and a professional progression. For example, in adulthood, Howard applied his designing and building experiences and skills in becoming an architect, and his brother George applied them as assistant manager at the San Lorenzo nursery, where he also added a childhood learning of horticulture and entomology. At the same time their younger brother Harry, who many people relied on to fix small electrical appliances in the internment camp in Arizona, and who at the age of 13 got a job as an electrician in the camp, later became an avionics engineer who exhibited and carried forward this same resourceful and creative spirit when he was part of the team at Mission Control in Houston that helped conceive methods to conserve power for the aborted Apollo 13 moon mission, "making the return flight possible for three astronauts."[16]

16 From *Boeing News*, April 28, 2000, p. 14.

Meanwhile, as the story of the raft unfolded, the roles of Howard and his compatriots were predictable. The tiny craft reached a point where it could be recognized and admired for what it was. One might suggest that crafts that negotiated stormy or calm seas of antiquity have existed as long as there has been both water and observant and thoughtful mariners. Howard told the story of the raft as he tells all of his stories, sharing characterizations of his family and friends and the qualities they exhibited, inquisitive, intuitive, and ingenuity. Always.

A later discussion with Howard prompted me to ask about the seaworthiness of their raft, to which Howard responded, "It floated."

Of course.

Rikimatsu Horii taught his sons by example as their childhood construction activities led to practical applications, and a professional progression. George became assistant manager at San Lorenzo nursery; Howard a principal for design in a Newark, N.J., architectural firm; Harry Director of Avionics at Rockwell; Robert City Engineer of Los Angeles; and Jim a technical illustrator and graphics designer. Back row, from left, George, Rikimatsu and Howard; front row, from left, Harry, Robert, and Jim.

In a Few Words

No poet, no writer
ever wrote
whole poems
entire essays…
worthy of
the writer's art
the concentration of
the reader's mind and
eye.

I've read a host of works
that came
so dangerously close…
that I've thought
"How extraordinary a writer..
what an unbelievable piece."

Only that writer
could have written
that stanza
those few words.

The Art of Noticing

It is the nature
of some folks
to practice
oblivion.

Surrounded as they are
by many species
of plants and animals
with which they have
so little familiarity.

At best,
all woodpeckers
are woodpeckers…
All hummingbirds
are hummingbirds…
and hawks,
hawks.

When one elects
to be inarticulate,
to wear permanent blinders…
to ignore the majesty
of the Great Blue Heron…

The artistry
of the Ruby Throated Hummingbird…

The rich coloration
of the Great Spangled Fritillary…

Where then,
is the awe?

Photo by Ken Horii

Civil Rights

That Light Comes Into the Soul
An Underlying Set of Truths

The Dr. Martin Luther King, Jr., Federal Building and U.S. Courthouse in Newark, N.J., one of the many architectural projects that Howard N. Horii worked on in his fifty years with the Grad architectural firm. Around the base of the sculpture *Head of Justice* by Diana K. Moore in front of the building is a poem by Mark Strand, U.S. Poet Laureate, 1990-1991, which reads:

WHEN JUSTICE DOES ITS PUBLIC PART
IT EDUCATES THE HUMAN HEART
THE ERRING HEART IN TURN
MUST DO ITS PRIVATE PART AND LEARN

That Light Comes Into The Soul

For years I marched as to a music in comparison with which the military music of the streets is noise and discord. I was daily inoxicated, and yet no man could call me intemperate. With all your science can you tell me how it is, and whence it is, that light comes into the soul?

—Thoreau[17]

There are people I've known whose role it has been to out-perform Prometheus[18] in support of those who were less fortunate. I've also been in the company of those who had power bestowed upon them and in their malfeasance abused those they were sworn to represent or protect. One summer, in the early 1960s, I was attending a seminar of the Collegiate Council for the United Nations at the University of Maryland. Speaking that evening was a Southern senator who, as I recall, had just returned from a fact finding mission to several emergent nations in Africa where the colonial presence was crumbling. The audience was mostly students, ranging from Ivy League schools, community colleges, and some historically black colleges.

---

17 Henry David Thoreau (1817-1862) American writer, philosopher, and naturalist.

18 In Greek mythology, among many other things Prometheus is known as a champion of mankind.

Many of the African American students had gathered in front of the podium. Our entertainment for that evening was Miriam Makeba,[19] a well-known South African musician and civil rights activist. Acknowledging the African American students in the audience, the senator smiled, nodded, and said something to the effect that he had just returned from Africa, noting what a wonderful people and experience it had been, but that unfortunately, they were not now, nor would they ever be able to govern themselves. The students were stunned into a deep silence by the provocative nature of his comments. Then, without pause or notice, they were joined by others, including myself, in an unplanned protest, all of us wanting in the worst way to disavow what the senator represented and his assumption of legitimacy.

When I taught high school in Nebraska, in the late sixties and early seventies, one of my courses was Black Studies. Among the posters inside my classroom covering the political spectrum was a poster of an African American man, Will Brown, whom a mob in Omaha had wrested from the police and other city officials. He was hanged and dragged behind a car before his body was placed on a funeral pyre during the Omaha Race Riot that occurred in late September 1919.

It was surprising for the students to learn that this could happen in Nebraska. As long as the tyranny of lynching against black people stood unimpeded there would be no justice to counteract bigotry and the impact of the robe, hood, and rope. Across America, some lynchings were treated almost as gala events with posters and placards distributed in surrounding counties, pictures portraying many smiling faces, women in gingham dresses, and small children playing, while holding American flags.

As an educational administrator in Iowa a decade later, I made several trips to Alabama and Mississippi in an attempt to employ teachers from historically black colleges and universities. This was the 1970s. My colleagues and I were faced with a host of issues concerning the preservice teachers. "How cold does it get in Iowa in the winter?" And more personally, "whom will I date?" The students we interviewed humbled us with their quiet dignity. Most of the students were the first in their families to attend college.

19 Miriam Makeba (1932-2008) Grammy Award-winning South African singer and civil rights activist.

Back home in Iowa, there were issues that proved much more daunting than we had ever assumed. I believed then and I believe now that public institutions have a responsibility to be diverse in their employment practices. Then, as now, there were many examples of classrooms where minority children were predominant and yet there were very few teachers, or staff members, representing the complete spectrum of society. The ferocity of a Midwestern winter and the relative lack of African American culture raised concerns in the new teachers about losing their religious ties, the separation from their families, and the possibility of intense social isolation. Our assumption that they would embrace and want employment in the north proved to be untrue.

One of my most notable trips during this time was to Jackson State University in Mississippi and neighboring Alcorn State University. To this day, my head resonates with the comment from one educator, "You need us more than we need you." This dean confronted us with the question, "Why would we trust you with our students?"

There was a steel, cold edge to his voice and not a hint of empathy. There was no reason for him to help us recruit his students, to have them move north to work in our schools. The warmest environment, the most loving and accepting people they would ever know were their teachers, mentors, friends, church members, and family where they already lived.

My answer was, "We are here." I added that our issues included the high incidence of minority children placed in special needs classrooms, and the unfortunate lack of minority teachers. When I traveled, I was always accompanied by a black colleague, a special needs teacher or a school board member. On one particular trip the colleague was Lou Porter, co-owner and president of KBBG, an African American public radio station in Iowa.

We arrived at the offices of Jackson State only to discover that the school was not in session, but the power of Southern hospitality instantly came into play. The dean instructed her staff, with kind consideration and haste, to round up student teachers in the area public schools to come listen to what we had to say about teaching positions in Iowa. I don't have the words to convey how close-knit Lou and I felt as we resolutely interviewed the students. They were so gracious and concerned about leaving Mississippi—about their families, and all their ties that we both knew we could not duplicate.

After our interviews at Jackson State we drove to nearby Alcorn State. Everything positive that transpired was forever overshadowed by what happened when we left. Our experience at Alcorn mirrored the hospitality that we experienced at Jackson. A bit of levity was added when one young man was puzzled that we did not know him. "I am the mascot for Alcorn State," he said. "Everyone in Mississippi knows who I am." It was early evening, the onset of dusk. As I unlocked the car, I found my colleague, Lou, visibly upset. I was puzzled and I asked if something had gone wrong in our meetings. Her reply was, "I am a black woman, alone in Mississippi, traveling with a white man." She told me that her husband had grown up in Jackson and that no one knew how many black bodies were buried in these swamps. She whispered, "We have a headlight out in the car and we will not make it home alive." We made it back to Jackson, but with little conversation between us.

The following afternoon, as I left the hotel where we were staying in Jackson, I noticed a man in military dress standing in front of the hotel windows. As I joined him I could see helicopters, military vehicles, and soldiers scurrying about. I wondered aloud about the activity. He explained there were NATO exercises going on, with several countries competing, and that he was in charge of the American troops. I looked closely at the American troops. There were scores of African American soldiers represented.

I then asked absent-mindedly, "How do you like Jackson?"

He responded with a racial epithet that horrified me especially considering that he was the officer in charge.

The next morning as we prepared to leave, I looked out the hotel window toward the Jackson State campus and could see several Klansmen picketing the candy store right off campus. When I inquired about their presence, no one I spoke to would offer a word of explanation. I reflected on the meaning of the Klan's presence so close to the campus. It didn't take many Klansmen for their presence to be felt.

Another trip I took in the early sixties was with an African American college friend, Milton Harrison. We were traveling Interstate 80 from Wayne State College in Nebraska to our respective homes in New York. We drove an old car Milton owned at the time. I had grown up in the Catskill Mountains of New York, intimately acquainted with the ways of mountain folk. Hunting, fishing, raising poultry, canning fruits, and vegetables were simply a way of life, but my world had forever changed dramatically when I found myself at the nexus of the civil rights movement.

Milton was from Brooklyn. He was an outstanding student and excelled as an athlete. He had won the Nebraska Golden Gloves Light Heavyweight Champion boxing title, slipping punches and working more as a dancer than a boxer. We ran together on our college cross country team. As students we found ourselves together in history and political science courses.

By the time we reached eastern Pennsylvania and western New Jersey, we were well into our routine, alternating payments for gas, driving and expounding on our youthful social senses. At one stop, several states removed from Nebraska, we ordered breakfast, changing menu items more than a few times, the waitress berating us with fiery words. We laughed and exchanged high fives. We were back home, where people let you know exactly what they thought.

As night approached, we both began to pay more attention to the road, mindful of the treacherous hills and sharp turns, beautiful, but a challenge especially for exhausted and sleep deprived drivers.

At one point, nearing the bottom of one of the long hills, I mentioned to Milton who was driving that he best slow down because a station wagon parked on the shoulder of the road appeared to me to be a highway patrol car. Milton said troopers didn't drive station wagons, but an officer from the vehicle soon pulled us over, menacingly waving a multi-cell flashlight to slowly peruse the interior of our car. He then instructed us to follow him.

We then followed him through winding hills, finally stopping at a country store in a sparsely settled area. We found ourselves being charged with speeding. Wearing bib overalls and little else, the Justice of the Peace inquired of us to the trooper.

"How much money do you think these boys have on them?"

The officer took our billfolds, removed our money and placed the money on the counter.

"How much money do you think it will take to get these boys out of our fine state?" the justice inquired.

This was followed by a meticulous counting of every penny, nickel, and dime. The officer outlined gas costs and tolls, not taking into account any other needs we might have. Leaving us with very little, the Justice of the Peace returned to us a meager amount and we were instructed to follow the officer back to the main highway. Bluntly saying, "we don't want this riffraff in our fine state and we want them to get the hell out of here." We left, but not forever. Milton was to return years later to become a highly respected president and chief executive officer of a New Jersey YMWCA.

Jimmie and Lou Porter of KBBG radio station in Waterloo, Iowa. Lou has been president and CEO of the station since 2007 when Jimmie died. Broadcasting since 1978, the radio station's motto is "communicate to educate" and is the largest African American owned and operated non-commercial radio station in Iowa.

Lou Porter's granddaughter Zoe Campbell recording her own radio show on KBBG "Zoe's Book Club with a Lotta Books."

Photo by Ken Horii

For many years Milton Harrison was president and chief executive officer of the YMWCA of Newark, N.J. and Vicinity. In 2005, The City of Newark, N.J. paid tribute to his outstanding leadership by dedicating "Milton Harrison Plaza" at the busy downtown intersection where the Newark Y is located.

An Underlying Set Of Truths

Lovejoy[20] has given his breast to the bullet for his part, and has died when it was better not to live. He is absolved. There are always men enough ready to die for the silliest punctilio; to die like dogs, who fall down under each other's teeth, but I sternly rejoice that one was found to die for humanity and the rights of free speech and opinion.

—Emerson[21]

There is an underlying set of truths that support a career as an educator. As I prepared to accept a position as a high school social studies/history teacher in Grand Island, Nebraska, in 1965, I found myself confronted with a set of social dynamics which increased the volatility of the teaching role. World War II professed to make the world safe for democracy, but as the United States was quick to find out, the war opened the eyes of women who assumed nontraditional roles in bomb factories, who became pilots to ferry the bombers to Europe, then went on to a broader, richer set of aspirations. Some African American men and women found Paris to be more inviting, a city that embraced them in a positive way, something that was generally

20 Elijah Lovejoy (1802-1837) An abolitionist who was killed by a pro-slavery mob in Alton, Illinois, in 1837.

21 Ralph Waldo Emerson (1803-1882) American essayist and poet.

not the case in their home country. Pearl Harbor had unleashed a tide of suspicion of Americans of Asian descent, confronting them with a racial bias that belied their generational accomplishments.

The "self-evident" truths in the Declaration of Independence about "Life, Liberty, and the pursuit of Happiness" cast a large net, encapsulating *all* Americans. Civil liberties became more than an ideal, like the force of a tsunami, justice once illuminated, raised the bar. As a teacher of African American studies, I saw the ugly truth was out of the bottle. Lynching was no anomaly. It was a control mechanism where black people were faced with whatever terror their oppressors could come up with, and punished for something fully known only to the oppressors who increasingly found themselves, with the impact of widespread news coverage, under a growing public scrutiny.

I was fortunate to have been offered a teaching position in Grand Island. Grand Island High School was large by regional standards. The district patrons valued education with strong programs in math, science, music, English, history, and vocational education. These were the times of competitive academic tracking, or ability grouping. My African American studies class was limited to eighteen students.

During this period, in the summer, I began working on my master's degree at Montana State University in Bozeman. The program was new, comprised of a cadre of students who were all history or English teachers and our program of studies followed an American Studies format. When I returned to Grand Island that fall I was asked to organize a course in African American studies. My African American studies program had a literary base, including among others, *The Confession of Nat Turner* by William Styron, *Manchild in the Promised Land* by Claude Brown, and *The Invisible Man* by Ralph Ellison. I became conscious of the scope of the program and its impact when the students delayed returning the books, with the most common excuse being, "My mom is still reading it."

One of the instructional processes followed each day was to examine the comments of major political figures ranging from political activist Angela Davis[22] to

22 Angela Davis (1944-) American political activist, scholar, and author.

segregationist Lester Maddox.[23] We discussed several major issues including civil rights, defense budgets and spending, welfare, and domestic policy and programs. We would place the topics on a political spectrum from the radical left to the reactionary right. At that time most candidates were moderate on many issues, swinging left or right depending on personal opinions. If ever there was a time when the politics of the era was illustrative of the extremes of the American viewpoint and the immense separation of many citizens from each other, this was such a time.

One of the acceptable tenets of the time was that for a political party and national candidate to be taken seriously, portions of their beliefs varied across the whole political spectrum. For example, Nelson Rockefeller's[24] ambitious urban renewal project in Albany, New York, was at the very least liberal, but his decision to quell the disturbance at Attica Prison, using all the power at his disposal, was much further to the right.

As our presidential discussions ebbed and flowed, third-party presidential candidate George Wallace[25] of Alabama brought his American party convention to Omaha, Nebraska, in March of 1968. Wallace was a Southern populist noted for his inflammatory comments on school integration, the peace movement, and any aspect of civil rights. He had an immense appeal to ultra-conservatives who would have blocked any attempts to extend basic civil rights specifically to the black community. As violence from the Klan grew, television pictures of the innocent victims had an immediate impact, driving home the inequities and injustices that prevailed.

With several colleagues and students, I traveled to Omaha to listen to Governor Wallace's speech. We wanted photos and notes to allow us to continue our political discussions in the classroom. Our experience was impacted by activities that occurred even before Wallace spoke. The air was heavily charged as Wallace had been bellicose in his attack on integration and civil rights. Anti-war activists were seen, in his eyes, as Communists. Wallace's speech was preceded by the

---

23 Lester Maddox (1915-1923) Governor of Georgia from 1967-1971, came to prominence as a staunch segregationist.

24 Nelson Rockefeller (1908-1979) A politically moderate Republican, Vice President of the United States from 1974-1977 and Governor of New York from 1959-1973.

25 George Wallace (1919-1998) Served four nonconsecutive terms as Governor of Alabama, remembered for his segregationist views that he renounced later in his life.

comments of a front man whose job it was to warm up the audience. Wallace emblazoned the conflict in the room by not appearing for over an hour from his published time. The speaker who opened for Wallace walked slowly to the podium. He was a tall, heavy, imposing figure. A small contingency of African American students had made their way to the area directly in front of the podium. The speaker opened his comments with a question, which as closely as I can remember, was stated: "Do many of you people believe that these black folks are here to listen to the wonderful message that Governor Wallace has traveled all the way from Alabama to share with you?"

The crowd, impassioned, came back with, "NO, NO!"

The speaker then inquired, "What should we do?"

The mob, inflamed, "Throw them out....throw them out!"

I cannot pretend to know what the black people in the front of the auditorium were planning to do. To a person, the Wallace supporters were not going to indulge their presence. I was in the balcony with the teachers and students from Grand Island. Two of the students roamed at will, trying to take photos. After the crowd's chant of, "Throw them out," the speaker interrupted, inciting them further.

For the first time that evening I became concerned for everyone's safety. The mob had grown surly. The folding chairs, which prior to the arrival of Wallace, seemed so innocuous or even church like were hoisted overhead and turned into weapons. The black people in the front of the auditorium were being attacked. Suddenly, from the back of the auditorium, an African American Marine, commanding in his military uniform, walked down the main aisle, accompanied by a pregnant woman. As they approached the front, chairs stopped in mid-air and were lowered. In the balcony we were in awe, silenced by the transformation from a possible blood bath, to relative order.

Recently, I went to a local grocery store and found myself in a conversation with a black man who was about my age. One of his relatives was a Tuskegee Airman.[26] His father had been murdered in Chicago. This man of about seventy years old had been an engineer on the railroad. He talked about his anger when he

26 Fought in World War II, were the first African American military aviators in the United States armed forces.

was younger, and how many of the things his father said to him had come back in a positive way. His father had talked about George Wallace, and Wallace's change in attitude toward black people later in his life. The George Wallace that came to Omaha in 1968 was a shrewd politician counting on his ability to incite a riot and enrage many Americans to support his agenda.

Mainstream news coverage of the Wallace convention at that time spoke mainly of the black people rioting in the Convention Center of Omaha that evening, but from my perspective, the black people were attacked. As I read much later, in an article by Michael Richardson,[27] of the scene inside the center, "police moved in to clear the aisles and suddenly the floor erupted in violence as Wallace supporters began hitting the trapped protestors with the metal chairs."[28]

In the aftermath of the Wallace Convention, newspaper headlines reflected the racial tension in America. Most often the headlines stated that it was the black people who rioted. However, in no account of that evening have I found an analysis of the words spoken from the podium which marshaled the Wallace supporters to violence, or of the role of the black Marine and his pregnant friend to redirect and to redefine the turn of events I remember.

On April 4th of that year, Dr. Martin Luther King, Jr.[29] was assassinated in Memphis, Tennessee, continuing the seemingly endless spasms of violence. The United States experienced many high profile assassinations: Medgar Evers,[30] John F. Kennedy,[31] and Robert Kennedy.[32] A peace march was held in Grand Island, Nebraska, in memory of Dr. King which some of my students and I attended. A foreign exchange student called crying, to tell me that he was sorry, as his host family would not allow him to attend. They were concerned about the potential for violence. I remember little children carrying palm branches during the march, as the policemen and firemen looked on.

---

27 Michael Richardson is a freelance writer and political consultant based in Boston. He writes about politics, law, nutrition, ethics, and music.

28 From "The Story of the Omaha Two, Part 3" *San Francisco Bay View National Black Newspaper,* June 25, 2011.

29 Dr. Martin Luther King, Jr. (1929-1968) Clergyman, activist, and prominent leader in the United States Civil Rights movement.

30 Medgar Evers (1925-1963) Civil rights activist from Mississippi, involved in efforts to overturn segregation at the University of Mississippi.

31 John F. Kennedy (1917-1963) 35th President of the United States, serving from 1961 until his assassination in 1963.

32 Robert F. Kennedy (1925-1968) Brother of John F. Kennedy, Democratic Senator from New York and noted civil rights activist.

An underlying set of truths we hold dear include the ideals of "Life, Liberty, and the pursuit of Happiness," for *all.* The availability of mass media brought the civil rights movement to every household. People would turn on their television sets and were suddenly confronted with a level of violence that decent people could neither accept nor tolerate, either for themselves, or for future generations. As Dr. King so eloquently stated when he wrote of the interrelatedness of all communities and states, "whatever affects one directly, affects all indirectly,"[33] which is something I'm reminded of over and over again.

33 From Dr. King's *Letter from Birmingham Jail*, which he wrote April 16, 1963. A year later, on July 2, President Lyndon B. Johnson signed The Civil Rights Act of 1964 and Dr. King was present at the signing of this landmark civil rights legislation.

Photo by Jeanette Hopkins

Road Trips

Being in Nature
Truth in the Rivers
In The Hearts of Children
There Was A Child Went Forth
Road Trips With Papa

Being In Nature

To him who in love of nature holds
Communion with her visible forms, she speaks
A various language; for his gayer hours
She has a voice of gladness, and a smile
And eloquence of beauty, and she glides
Into his darker musings with a mild
And healing sympathy...
—William Cullen Bryant[34]

A deep affinity for nature occurs as an individual walks or lies upon the earth, cultivating a relationship with bogs, prairies, rock formations, and listening to the voices in the wind. Listening to stories of sacred elders, local anecdotes, folk myths, and the complexity of community also provide a natural connection. The Iowa Loess Hills area is a unique land form, bordering the Missouri River north from near the Iowa-Missouri border to the picturesque town of Akron, Iowa. Within this region's boundaries are patches of undisturbed prairie, groves of bur oaks, cat steps, and deep inclusions.

The Loess Hills wear seasonal faces—the rugged determination of winter, spring with its revered prairie pasque flowers, summer with its succession of prairie grasses and cone flowers. As summer gives way to fall, the Loess Hills exhibit

34 William Cullen Bryant (1794-1878) American poet and editor. Bryant wrote this poem, "Thanatopsis," while he was in his late teens, and it was published in *The North American Review* in September, 1817. In a letter to Bryant and his father, the editors declared it, "the very best poetry that has been published in this country."

faces of deep bronze, every tint of brown imaginable along with splashes of peach. Many plant species stand out for the tilt of their step, the angular form of sumacs, the three pronged turkey step of giant bluestem, the rugged form of bur oaks among them.

I initiated a practice of "road trips" to broaden the base of experiences for myself, my grandchildren, and others in our environment. These excursions are part road trip with quiet observations, walking and recording what is encountered. Some observations are simply seasonal, even predictable. The first Mourning Cloak butterfly encountered amidst the fading banks of snow in a county park allows us to not so much go looking for something but to accept what nature serves up. Very few trips occur without our observing white tail deer in their seasonal dress—the early season emergence of shaggy velvet horns, the frenetic behavior of the rut, or finding large flocks of wild turkey roosting in the tops of cottonwoods particularly when storms are imminent.

One fall, the focus for much of my activity was on photographing deer. Three of the largest bucks we photographed were within the city limits of Sioux City. One of these episodes unfolded when one of my grandsons and I were hiking to Turtle Lake within the confines of Stone State Park. As we walked with our walking sticks toward the lake, an eight point buck erupted from a briar patch next to the trail. His line of flight was directly toward us. As he passed, I pulled the young man to me and softly instructed him not to move. As the buck passed, it was evident that he might not have seen us. The object of his attention was a doe standing to our right, up the hill. Over a period of fifteen minutes the doe passed us, followed by the buck. They passed several times, running back and forth on the flat, before disappearing from our view.

After this we stopped to build a small hut, one of many activities my grandchildren have come to own and request, laying poles, intertwined with sinewy branches and weighted down with sticks and leaves. Typically when we complete a hut, we gather up our backpacks and materials to move on. On this trip we heard a rustling on the flat above us and were surprised to find the buck watching us, "taking our picture" we wondered?

In spite of the hunting pressure required by the Department of Natural Resources to manage the size of Iowa's deer population, Iowa continues to produce trophy bucks. Another time, during one fall afternoon, I left home alone with the intent of testing a new camera and initiating a road trip. My first subject was a large doe lying next to a blue spruce about sixty yards up a hill. She was a most distinctive doe with a light coat and angular neckline. I took several photo shots then left. For some reason I felt a need to return. When I returned a buck stepped out from behind the spruce, just behind was the doe. He had used the tree to shield himself from my view. I believe the buck had been within yards of the doe as I photographed her, and only stepped out when he thought I had left.

On another road trip, this time without a camera, we were treated to an interesting, but perplexing set of white tail buck behaviors. The deer were well within the city limits, in close proximity to busy roads. Two young bucks, a spike horned and prong horned were feeding in the company of a more well developed six horn eastern count. The two smaller deer began sparring-pushing each other. This went on for several minutes, interrupted by brief feeding activity. The two young bucks again began sparring-pushing on each other—their heads riding on the grass—awkward and unconvincing. As they struggled, the larger buck stood several paces away watching the scenario play out. After a while, the larger buck intruded, pushing first on one of the smaller bucks, then the other. His actions forced the smaller deer to raise their heads ever so slightly before locking horns. These episodes were interspersed with quiet periods when the bucks stopped to graze. The instructive role played out by the larger deer was something I had never observed before. The closest I had come was watching two large bucks in what looked like practice rounds in midsummer at a Nebraska wildlife refuge. Social activity within small groupings of deer serves to define roles and behaviors much as it does in human communities.

As we navigate our road trips, I am often reminded of words of Thoreau, "in Wildness is the preservation of the world" or as Gary Snyder[35] says, "our relation to the natural world takes place in a place and it must be grounded in information and experience." These spots on the earth are memorialized in thought and

35 Gary Snyder (1930-) American poet, essayist, lecturer, and environmentalist.

writings, in the art and attachment we call home. What is heartening is when my younger grandchildren call my attention to what they have seen in nature and are able to verbalize their feelings of attachment such as the richness of habitat, the ability to discern the connection between the presence of certain plants and animals in different settings becomes the internalization of our appreciation of *being in nature.*

Every specie we take the time to observe enriches our understanding of our environment. In many instances there are more opportunities to observe several species today than we would have been afforded decades ago. Wild turkeys, coyotes, and white tail deer have proven to be very adaptive, even resilient to the ever changing conditions of the environment. I've encountered coyotes in early morning sprinting out of a larger city along Interstate 80. Wild turkeys abound in many habitats in prodigious numbers, in suburbs, inside the city as well as the country in spite of having once been hunted to near extinction.

Wild turkeys sometimes graze like herds of bison flowing over open prairie, upon heavily wooded areas, and neighborhood lawns. As we observe them, a grandchild's inquiry is always "can they fly?" One wintry evening, under a heavy snow warning, we drove west out of Sioux City, past Briar Cliff College. A couple of miles further west, we looked down across a meadow and spotted over seventy turkeys riding out the storm in the crowns of several large cottonwood trees which served as their protector from predators and the deep snows.

In art and literature not too many decades ago, the terms sublime and beautiful represented very different faces of nature. A painting which portrayed a sailing ship being battered and driven before the storm represented the wildness inherent in nature. Many pastoral paintings represented beauty as the dominant theme. For our road trips, Midwestern weather is often a form of both of those terms. We are fortunate in these times, that weather forecasting is a fairly reliable science, yet thunder storms that become tornadic, result in tragic conditions even for those who have been diligent.

Very few animals represent the full spectrum of dangerous behaviors as do white tail deer, running the gambit of being perceived as "Bambi" to an extremely dangerous wild animal. Don't believe me? Well, particularly during the rut, deer behavior is erratic and unpredictable. I once initiated a conversation with environmental friends about things in nature that have terrified them, including confrontations involving deer. A story aired on television last year concerning a young man who was involved in a taming experience as the deer were in a fenced in enclosure. Each day he would push the boundaries, hand feeding the deer, in hopes of encouraging a relationship. He was killed when he was attacked by a young buck as the tip of the rack punctured his skull.

Common to the experience where people were out in nature and became fearful, was the feeling of being alone and not in a social context. Because these outings of mine, or when with my grandchildren, do not involve the intent to be out for a prolonged period of time, we slip out with a camera and binoculars but little else. One evening I was settled in on a wooded hillside, crisscrossed by game trails. It was in the late fall, the days were shortening, and dusk arrived quickly accompanied by a decided chill. I remained in place until I could no longer see the hillside. Gathering my belongings—a journal, camera, binoculars—I began the short trek down the hill to the car. As I walked, I began to develop an uneasy feeling of not being alone. The rustle of leaves and swish of grasses softened my footsteps. At first, when I stopped to listen, I was greeted with a deafening silence. As the intensity of my senses heightened, so did the knowledge that I was being shadowed. But, I wondered, by what? Normally I would be wearing a sheath knife, and often I carried a walking stick, but this time I had nothing. Even though these instruments would have proved to be impractical, and probably not helpful, they gave me a feeling of being able to protect myself. All of this added to the growing awareness that although I was well prepared to observe nature, I was in every sense very ill prepared to be *in* nature.

The source of my consternation soon became clear. A deer, probably one that routinely traveled the game trails unimpeded, had encountered something with which it was most uncomfortable. In the fall when the trees have dropped their leaves and the trails are dry, the deer have little fear of predators. Snow and hunting seasons change that equation. This deer used every defensive measure I have ever experienced. She snorted, grunted, stamped her feet, and thrashed at the bushes. Moving parallel to me, I made my way down the hill. I was struck by the intensity and duration of her feigned attack.

Just as a familiarity with classical literature during childhood is important, so too is the involvement with nature that we can provide to our children and grandchildren. Well-written and well-illustrated books provide social and environmental lessons, but there is another kind of cultural literacy that can only come through a personal involvement with the natural world, by directly "being in nature" which road trips and nature excursions can provide. Through these experiences, children and adults alike, develop a deep association with a much broader concept of community, the act of participating in and becoming part of the fabric of interdependent parts, plants, animals, people, which, in relationship to children, frame much of a child's caring and sense of well being for the rest of their lives.

Early in his career Emerson wrote "no art can exceed the mellow beauty of one square rood of ground in the wood this afternoon." The opportunity to be in nature is slipping away, as more and more of our citizens live in cities. There is a pernicious cost to our society when children are isolated from real play. The complexity of culture unfolds when the explosive qualities of observing migrating geese, the community woodchuck, and the irregular visitation of the sandhill cranes impact human emotions. If nature in its darkest hours is treated as something to be feared or needing to be tamed, it leads to greater isolation and loneliness. Coming to nature is a humanizing experience, enriching our lives to a deep sense of art, culture, moral responsibility, and the larger community of inclusiveness.

Late Summer Happenings

The gardens have gone
ragged, coneflowers and
daisies lay prostrate…

    Flattened by the wind,
    hail, and rain of heat
    induced thunderstorms.

Blackened sunflower heads
    bend downward, as if
    watching the earth.

There is a pronounced
urgency in the feeding and
habits of the goldfinches…

    and the butterflies.

One day soon, the heat
and humidity will be slapped
senseless by the harsh cold
edge of an insistent night
    and the incursion

of cold arctic air.

Impending Darkness

Trees overhang
the long abandoned
rutted logging road.
When first the shade pervades the undercover,
the transformative voices of
crickets and frogs usher in the night.

Soon the bobcats caterwaul
from the hollows
and the ledges…
moonlight filters down to the forest floor…

His mother's last words
had been
"Be home before dark"…
As his pace quickened,
so did the missteps…

As each foot touched the ground
wrenched as it settled
on upturned rocks…twigs…
And the anticipation of affirmation

there was none.

As he ran, branches
slapped at his arms,
his face.
grabbed
at his ankles…adding to his despair.

His pulse raced incoherently.
Fear wracked his body…sounds from the forest…
ominous, ever close.

He ran awkwardly....a marionette yanked about
on taut strings.

Ahead, he could see the clearing...
the pathway bathed in moonlight.
As he cleared the logging road,
he began to walk and breathe...rhythmically.

Nothing about this night was new.
Even as it occurred, it was imagined.
After dinner each evening, he would
find himself realizing that there was
no way home except through the darkness.

Old Settler Prairie Cemetery

In every way
the spot is ordinary
the gravestones
lack pretension.

The access roads
are dust
fine loess soil
meandering roads

Families
laid to rest,
dates following
upon dates
in tight succession

The land,
is appropriately arid
prairie flowers
nudge against
the markers
quaint, dainty.

Epidemics made tidy,
yet-evoking
a deep empathy
for the dignity
nature and time have bestowed.

An Ominous Cloud

One cloud freed itself from the
conformity of a lifeless sky,
in the light of day,
children found themselves staring skyward
being asked to find patterns
a dog, an airplane, or a gladiator…

In the darkening sky, the nonconforming
cloud rose above the prairie…as the heat
of a very hot July day expressed itself…
rushing upward, expanding into a glorious prism of
light…configured by the descending sun…

As the cloud towered ever higher,
lightning exploded from its crest,
descending between what had been invisible crevices…
thunder rolled outwardly,
expanding aggressively.

Below the clouds
the children who had found figures in them..
and now rested…
were jarred into a full state of alert.
Mumbling a prayer, their parents oft repeated…
as they lay them down to sleep.

If I should die before I wake…

The ominous cloud let out with
a shattering roar…
one which disturbed the soul of the night…
awakened the children,
and then their parents,
who offered such profound solace…

"Don't worry, dear, it's only God bowling."

Truth In The Rivers

"Beauty is truth, truth beauty,"—that is all
Ye know on earth, and all ye need to know.
—John Keats[36]

I would offer that to experience nature is to open ourselves to its rejuvenating powers, as well as to awaken our political and social consciousness. Out and about on a late fall afternoon, the chill hints at the incursion of winter. The dark faced scudding clouds wrapping themselves over and around the crest of hills, darkening the valleys, opening the mind's eye to vistas and natural occurrences, awakening the senses.

Infused in nature we find ourselves liberated from the confines and limitations of society. Driving Interstate 80, west from Des Moines, Iowa, the topography is hilly, with curves which disappear in the fog and mist. Traffic on the interstate adds treacherous overtones, particularly as semi-truck drivers compete with a host of people to get somewhere by an appointed time. I seek interludes where I can drive and yet experience natural occurrences. Nature erupts on the scene, overriding the monotony of the road and the hypnotic conditions it can induce. Sometimes there is the harvest being completed, or hunters in the fields searching through the tattered remnants of habitat.

---

36 John Keats (1795-1821) English poet.

Just west of Stuart, Iowa, rain spattered against the windshield defying the rhythmic beating of the windshield wipers. As I was negotiating a particularly tight turn I was confronted by a flock of Canada Geese sliding over an embankment, crossing over my line of sight, within yards. I could see into their eyes and feel their communal effort as they lifted out and over the car. These geese were heading south in a pelting downpour, aided by the intemperate consistency of a northwest wind pushing them along. Whatever we have conditioned our eyes to anticipate, to lift out of the complexity of patterns nature presents, has the potential to be recorded as experience. The geese appeared in a sudden moment but remained riveted in my mind for an expanse of time.

As the journey continued, the hillside immediately to the north was rich with color, not as seen in the prism of summer but a product of the waning hours of fall and the closeness of winter. The prairie grasses flashed a deep rust, variations of brown closing in the short grasses with a rich yellow leaning towards orange. Overhead in a bush inclined against a fence, a scruffy rough legged hawk held on to an uppermost branch, its feathers buffeted by the force of the wind and rain. This segment of hillside preceded by dark grasses and followed by the same had managed to retain its rich colors and confirmation in this season of decay.

When the temperatures of fall are moderate, the geese and the hawks have little reason to move on. Hawks have adapted to seasonal farming activities as the crops are removed. Moles, mice, rabbits, and other critters become vulnerable to the hunting hawks and other predators. Several species of hawks now utilize all form of trees, bushes, even mile markers as viewing posts from which to observe their hunting domain. This day, the low cloud ceiling forced the hawks down on low perches. At one point a red tail hawk plummeted into a deep ditch alongside the road. His wings and tail feathers extended as he rode the nuances of the wind down upon his unsuspecting prey.

American kestrels often perch low on mile marker signs bringing them alarmingly close to the road. Few hawks have the intrinsic deep beauty of these lovely creatures, with their dark sideburns, patches of grey and burnt orange. Once a naturalist friend, Duane Kent, an environmentalist and educator from Aurelia, Iowa, related an experience he had with a bluebird box. He was working his bluebird trail, checking the boxes for intruders such as snakes or mice, to assure that the boxes were hospitable for bluebirds, when, to his consternation, he encountered a box stuffed and stacked with the carcasses of several species of colorful birds, absent their heads. At first he was deeply puzzled. Nothing in his field experiences pointed to a specific culprit. After careful examination, he spotted a kestrel patrolling the clearing on which the trail bordered. He had discovered his culprit.

Crossing Iowa on Interstate 80 in late fall showcases that wildness is a natural state of which mankind is a part and has been for thousands of years. Specie interdependence is reflected in every turn. In late November, when the snow geese come to the DeSoto National Wildlife Refuge, so do the predators, coyotes, bald eagles, great horned owls, and a variety of hawks. Many geese hunters would swear that, as the lace curtain formations of snow geese arrive, they fly high before reaching the boundary of the Refuge and ascending. According to the hunters, the snow geese seem to know just where the boundary is.

The long trip across Iowa on Interstate 80 is seldom treated as memorable, but at one stop, just off the interstate near dusk, I noticed a large buck who was bedded down under some trees. I also noticed a couple who seemed to have followed me most of the day from place to place. The man looked at me and asked what I was looking at, I pointed out the buck. Turns out that while I had been photographing flowers, grasses, vistas, and wildlife all day they had not observed much at all. The man commented to me, "We haven't seen anything all day." Having come with the intent of taking in what nature had to offer, I had accumulated numerous photos, notes and memories.

After this trip, I was visiting with a local naturalist on how powerful and evocative it is to observe an American bald eagle in flight. Eagles fly powerfully. I call it rowing through the air with strong methodical strokes. Frequently when I'm driving along the Missouri River within the Sioux City, Iowa, city limits, I find eagles perched in trees close both to the interstate and the river. Eagles have become a source of inspiration to those who enjoy watching them. They have thrived in part because of the banning of pesticides which threatened their existence but also because they have few natural predators. Several years ago north of Cherokee, Iowa, in a county park I photographed an eagle perched in a cottonwood tree flanked on each side by a great horned owl. Horned owls are eagles only true predators.

I do believe we see what we prepare ourselves to see. Henry David Thoreau characterized himself as a student of snow banks. The poignancy of his comment was that the beauty that sustains us is often close at hand. Crossing Iowa with an inclination towards its natural beauty confirms the variability in the topography of the land and the subtle variations in the colors of the grasses as the seasons change.

As I study the landscape, I become more conscious of how rivers and streams define the character of communities. What many northern Plains states have in common are rivers of notoriety, the Dismal and Platte rivers of Nebraska, the Missouri and Mississippi rivers which are associated with many states including Iowa, as well as a myriad of smaller but distinctive rivers and streams throughout the region. Every single one of these rivers is a huge part of the migratory route of the sandhill cranes, snow geese, and other water fowl.

Deeply associated with the rivers would be the properties of the land itself, the quality of life, history and culture of its people. Several thematic streams course through my writings and poems. Rivers and streams offer glimpses of perspective on human rights, environmental stewardship, our ideals of inclusiveness and justice, and the need to "teach our children well." Bringing children, and ourselves, to nature provides a sense of belonging and a personal ethic which can guide behavior.

"Truth in the Rivers" in this essay, and throughout this book as well, unfolds through essays, poems, and artistic renderings, supporting a level of empathy which encapsulates our commitment to teach our children well, to use every example of rejection and social isolation to define the standards that a democratic society will not accept. Thoreau wrote of his greatest regret that he might die and discover that he never lived. To have lived is to have experienced the ideals of connections, as we interact with each other and with our communities, across age, gender, racial differences, and with the artistry of life.

This midwestern farm scene offers a peaceful respite from a long drive on Interstate 80.

In The Hearts Of Children

Photo from author's personal journal

They are of a simplicity always so refined that there is no touch of coarseness in them; with their perfect naturalness they are of a delicate artistry which will take the young children unaware of its perfection, and will only steal into their consciousness perhaps when they are very old children. Some may never live to feel the art, but they will feel the naturalness at once.

—William Dean Howells[37]

Recently I read a biography of J.D. Salinger[38] which spoke to Salinger's attachment to children, attributing to them a closeness to God which allowed them to love more purely. The world of adults is composed of a complex system of social mechanisms, class standards, pseudo religious beliefs, and economic determinisms which serve to separate them from one another, creating barriers to civil discourse, and acceptance, alienating individuals from each other and leading them to distrust their own senses.

37 William Dean Howells (1837-1920) American author. From *Hans Andersen's Fairy Tales and Wonder Stories.* Illustrated by Louis Rhead and Introduction by W.D. Howells.

38 J.D. Salinger (1919-2010) American novelist, author of *The Catcher in the Rye*. From *J.D. Salinger, A Life*, by Kenneth Slawenski.

Young children on the other hand play with absolute abandonment, utilizing their imaginations to fill whatever void that might occur, be it the absence of toys or formal structure. In other words, their world is magically populated. They are free to explore emergent language, to utilize sounds, and invented phrases to accompany the cacophony in their brain (for which there is neither lexicon nor dictionary). They have a special affection reserved for whom or what it is: Mom, Dad, blanket, teddy. Most children have a private language which becomes home-base for the structural language they will carry into the world of becoming an adult.

The delight of children was put on display one afternoon when our oldest granddaughter, Taylor, who was a toddler at the time, led my wife and me on an active exploration of pre-language. In a Midwest department store she launched into a highly expressive discourse, complete with elaborate hand gestures, facial expressions, and vocalizations. It was all so invigorating that before long a small crowd of adults had gathered, stopping what they were doing in order to become part of the expressive world she had created. Children often share with older adults, their grandparents, and other seniors, a sense of awe and set of sensitivities which does not occur to their parents and younger adults, who are often preoccupied with the surreal functionality of adulthood.

Children can also have a special relationship with pets, and inanimate objects. In our home we have several metal rabbits. At some point, they have been a focal point of the play activity of all of our very young grandchildren. In spite of the weight and hard metal qualities, they assume, for the children playing with them, a warm sense of friendship, affirmation, and engagement. Using their imagination, healthy children have the capability to do this and wise adults know that it would be unhealthy to discourage or take away the "realness" of the world that children create for themselves.

In children, their imagination, like nature itself, provides certain assurances. I share with Chellis Glendinning[39] and other deep ecologists a concern for what happens when people are separated from the assurances of nature. I've actively sought to devise activities which involve our grandchildren in that broader society

39 Chellis Glendinning, PhD (1947-) European American author of *When Technology Wounds,* licensed psychotherapist, and political activist.

which encapsulates natural places, taking road trips and embarking on all kinds of outdoor activities, even using pocket knives to carve walking sticks for making their way through our explorations. As they wander, they collect all kinds of small objects, leaves, stones, dead insects, to delightfully share with their grandmother and their parents at the end of these experiences.

Very young children refer to these artifacts as "natures." The relative randomness of children's explorations facilitate involvement with the unexpected, be it a decaying leaf or a small stone. The act of selecting an object from an assortment of possibilities affirms the child's membership in a larger community. Byrd Baylor[40]wrote of this in her children's book, *The Other Way to Listen*. She speaks of a small lizard taking the entire day to find the "perfect" rock to sun himself.

Unfortunately, the wildness that Thoreau espoused as the hope for the preservation of the world, is not universally valued through much of society today. Wilderness preserves, along with national, state, and county parks have experienced deep economic cuts while the demand for accessibility has increased from a public divided on the function they serve. For our grandchildren, not only my own, but everyone's the nature centers of regional states have assumed critical roles for the integration of natural communities sense of well-being, belonging, and responsibility.

For example, one spring day my wife, several of our grandchildren, and I were hiking in the Iowa Loess Hills at the Dorothy Pecaut Nature Center. Remnants of snow nestled in the inclusions, against the base of trees. A darkened apparition lifted from the forest floor, flitting in front of us before landing on the trail. It was an early harbinger of spring, a Mourning Cloak. Our grandson Cole followed the butterfly, bending down near its resting point on the trail. Art and nature share the impactful moment of recognition. "This is beautiful," was his insight and personalization. I have a photo of him, bent down, supporting himself against a tree, oblivious to everything but the butterfly. This brief excursion led us into the woods with which we were familiar yet allowed us yet another new experience.

---

40 Byrd Baylor (1924-) Naturalist and author, lives and writes in Arizona, presenting images of the Southwest and an intense connection between the land and the people.

The sign board at the entrance became one of the first group of words our grandchildren could read and ushered them into this natural community.

Recently, one of our regional nature centers completed a major renovation project. The immediate impact was stunning, bringing the voices, sounds, and forms of nature to the public. The impact on children and their families was evident in the intensity of participation as they identified old standards such as a honey bee colony and experienced the positive effect of other exhibits as they were brought into greater proximity. The fish tank, now clear, exhibits native species familiar to most adults and are now part of the base experience for younger children. Experientially, there are feeding stations and gardens which attract many species of butterflies and birds, providing visitors ample opportunity to watch garter snakes and toads as they patrol the gardens. The journey from learning what a bird is, to what a woodpecker is, to what is a downy woodpecker are readily available. The Dorothy Pecaut Nature Center staff, professionals, volunteers, and interns enrich the social experience and instill a greater joy of learning by engaging all who enter.

Along its myriad of trails, nature reveals herself in substantive ways. Acorns and leaves of a variety of oaks, nuthatches, chickadees, and a wide range of woodland birds enliven the senses. Any walk is liable to present tracks of opossums or raccoons, a sighting of white tail deer, or wild turkeys, while holding out the possibility of sighting the reclusive bobcat. The opportunities to examine stewardship, the benefits of being quiet and observant in nature are paramount. Culture is learned, but nature paints with a broad palette. We explain to our grandchildren about "being prepared" and how the joy of observing comes in small doses. A daddy long-legs spider crosses our path, the croaking voice of a white breasted nuthatch is first heard and then finally found.

When we visited the Dorothy Pecaut Nature Center in the past, our grandchildren measured their own personal growth against the poster of the wing-span of several species of birds. Immediately after renovation, we discovered the bird exhibit was gone. In fact, our very youngest grandchild stated, "Papa, I can't find the bird poster." Several days later, we returned and found the poster remounted, balancing the powerful impact of the renovation against a sense of continuity and sacredness of place. This exhibit had become a part of how our grandchildren perceived themselves. As we discussed the reappearance of the bird poster, we found ourselves at the center of a small circle of folks all expressing their delight that the poster was back where it belonged.

These centers are part of our perspective on place. We watch Canada Geese raise their young, noticing specie behaviors, the role of the sentinels, how they often swim in a line with a parent at the front and back. And we watch with care a mother raccoon as she brings her young to feed. The seasonal faces of nature, the moments of insight and experience when entering the natural community in a quiet way all provide a depth and enrichment.

Children learn from nature. They also learn from their own imagination, particularly when encouraged by caring adults. In essence, the inventive world of small children is not that different from the world of aspirations and dreams of young adults, or for that matter the world of nontraditional older students.

There is a common perspective that children today are difficult to teach because they have short attention spans. We have not found this to be true. What I have found is that when adults are actively engaged with the learning of children, attention is not an issue. Learning is a social experience, and I think children can often learn well beyond the labels that educators and others sometimes place on them. When children are involved in a meaningful activity and an adult is similarly engaged, they each exhibit an almost limitless attention span.

I recently spent a morning with all of my grandchildren culling sticks from a variety of wooded areas that we thought might be carved into walking sticks. In the afternoon, we gathered at the patio in the backyard. Each child selected from a collection of pocket knives to prepare his or her own personal walking stick. Stripping the sticks, removing the nub of branches, the sticks were completed. Sometimes old splits were filled with wood filler, sanded, and varnished. By evening, decorative applications were made with leather strips, feathers, and beads, truly creating masterpieces of imagination. Our activity took the entire day, but time flew by and the children worked hard, encouraged by the tools of the trade and inspired by the variety of nature and creativity.

As they carved and decorated their personal walking sticks together they were learning what it means to be in a broader community which enriches and sustains interest for the rest of their lives. All eleven of our grandchildren—Taylor, Haley, Jordan, Sydney, Peyton, Mackenzie, Cole, Kaden, Chloe, Keegan, and Micah made walking sticks, celebrating their love of nature.

As young children grow, engaging other children, they become more independent and at the same time more vulnerable. The walking stick experience is powerful because it occurs out of doors. Sticks need to be found and selected individually. The acts of cleaning, carving, learning to work with tools such as pocket knives, saws, and sandpaper in a shared experience prepares children for similar life challenges ahead. Children recognize that when they are encouraged in walking about, learning the names of flora and fauna as well as place names, they begin to experience the joy of learning and to develop their own personal ability to initiate projects from road trips and walkabouts when looking for wildlife. They initiate such activities while at the same time articulating a set of behavioral ethics.

Experience has shown that individuals who have several mentors grow in their proficiency as students of learning and demonstrate responsibility for helping others. Mark Twain[41] and Charles Dickens[42] are two authors in addition to Salinger and the poets Henry Wadsworth Longfellow[43] and Walt Whitman[44] who were drawn to the idea of the lives of young people as characters in a much larger universal drama. Over and over I am then reminded of the lessons we both teach and can learn from children.

41 Mark Twain (1835-1910) American writer.

42 Charles Dickens (1812-1870) English novelist.

43 Henry Wadsworth Longfellow (1807-1882) American poet.

44 Walt Whitman (1819-1892) American poet.

Yearning

I miss
walking sticks
green snakes slithering
through wet grass...

I long for salamanders
the plump black ones
the smaller orange ones,
that lived beneath
the rotted form
of ancient hemlocks.

Photo by Jeanette Hopkins

Late Fall Grasshoppers

Up until now,
the grasshoppers
have held to the security
of numbers.

Whatever their missteps
their adversaries
would have to contend

With their
jumps and glides
distancing themselves
deep within the nap
of grasses.

Patterned within
the antiquity
of their specie
a sensing of the end
of this, their season.

For reasons I don't understand
they plump up,
massive in form

Like grandparents
who once danced
lithe in line
and spirit.

Forest Sojourn

So you walked through the forest
Did you notice
That the flowers were not perfect
That the sky was pale towards gray
And that the wind had no direction

So you walked through the forest
Did you smell the loam
And feel the small rocks
Interspersed with tracks of ants
And twigs that rot in random fashion

So you walked through the forest
Did you hear the sounds that mice make
In anticipation of a nocturnal commitment
The shadow of a hawk
And the veinal structure of a rotted leaf

So you walked through the forest
Did you feel the giving away of spider webs
Introspective shy and unobtrusive
The bending of the grass
And the forlorn cry of the native one?

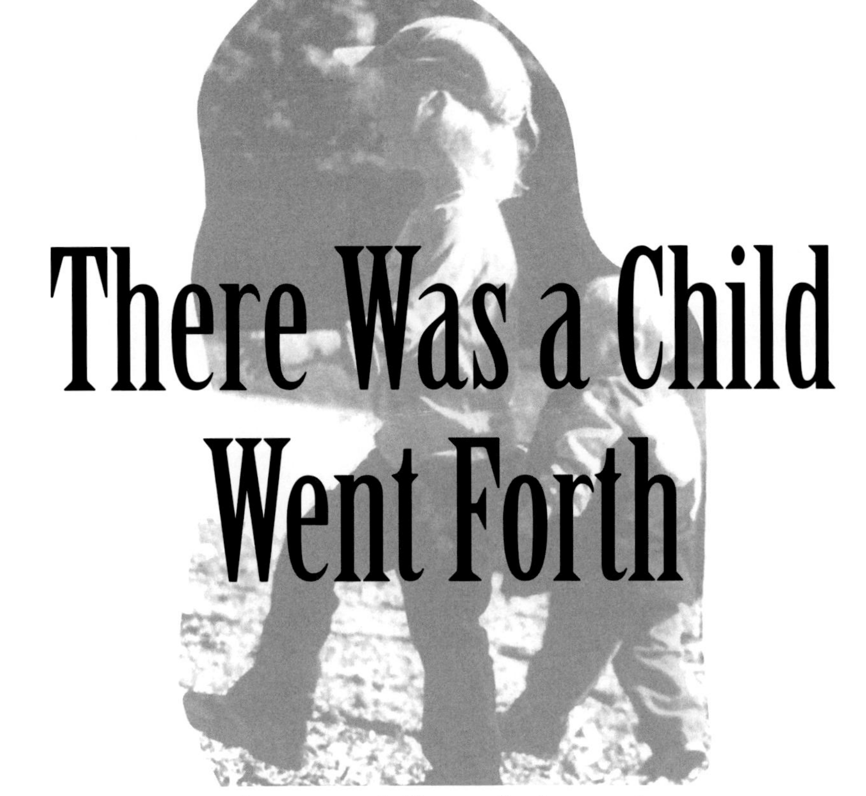

There Was a Child Went Forth

Photo from the author's personal journal.

There was a child went forth every day;
And the first object he look'd upon, that object he became;
—Walt Whitman[45]

As I carried Micah, one of my young grandchildren around a restaurant that had mounted fish, deer, and moose on the walls, I talked quietly to him, pronouncing the common name of each. He would give the names back to me with great pride in his voice, as the naming of any person, place, or thing creates such understanding in a child.

One day, after we had departed his daycare center in Sergeant Bluff, Iowa, we scurried down to Onawa, Iowa, with the hope of finding open patches in the waterway ice that might host Canada Geese and several species of ducks, including mallards and mergansers. On the way, we spotted red-tailed hawks perched high in the trees and on the lesser promontories of our route. I said to him, "Look, a hawk," and he mimicked my delight. His attention to language was amazing to me as I noticed how he searched my face for advanced understanding.

45 Walt Whitman (1819-1892) American poet.

When Micah comes to our house in the evening, one of his initial rituals is to gesture to the bookcase which hosts a large number of children's books. He has a verbal list of his favorites which includes *Hattie and Fox* by Mem Fox[46] (not at all a surprise as Mem Fox is his Nana's favorite author). This book meets several of the literary criteria that my wife and I deem important. For us, a favorable child response is the very most important. Young children are imbued with anthropomorphism which prescribes human qualities to animals. Children find animals, when portrayed in children's books, as friends they grow closer to with each reading. In *Hattie and the Fox*, a story evocative of *The Little Red Hen,* each farm animal exhibits adult behaviors that allude to the idea that, "they simply don't care." Children get this point early on in the story and at times, early on in their own lives.

Another classic Micah loves is *The Teddy Bears' Picnic.* The words were an original musical score written in the early 1900s.[47] The book is often sung to our grandchildren. Children's picture books contain so few words that the crafting of rhyme, rhythm, and repetition and the selection of individual words becomes an artistic endeavor.

As with any body of literature, there is a body of work which supports its heart and soul. This is true of children's literature. Although each individual who knows children's literature well might have his/her own list of favorites, each child emerges from the experience of the read aloud being initiated into the powerful world of literacy. In *The Teddy Bears' Picnic*, young readers bring their own verbal language, words that astound adults for their creative nuances. In the case of Micah, his word for teddy bear has been simply, "Bop-bo," which he also used for the teddy bears he sleeps with at night, or encounters in other books. Characters in children's books are carried forward through the words of the author as well as the representation by the illustrator, but it is the child who brings the characters to life.

I could write a book about what transpires in the experience when an adult holds a child on his/her lap while reading a book out loud. The child becomes both transfixed and transformed, experiencing the warmth of human interaction

46 Mem Fox (1970-) Australian children's book author.

47 A popular children's song with a melody written by American composer John Walter Bratton in 1907, and lyrics added by Irish songwriter Jimmy Kennedy in 1932.

nurtured through a familiarity with a story and its pacing and its characters. In our family we teach our grandchildren to respect the book itself. Children and grandchildren are given as gifts hard bound delightfully textured real books over paperback or technologically altered ones.

Another good example of a children's book is *Good Night Moon* by Margaret Wise Brown[48] which appeals to all young children. The book is quieting, as the words and pictures bid, "Good Night, Room … Good night cow jumping over the moon"… ending with "Good night noises everywhere." Children's books invite the powerful forces of imagination into a world where literature, stories, and songs are crucial to a child's sense of well being.

Wise Brown's simple text is brilliant, creating an environment where each child is completely absorbed into an understanding of his/her connection to the scenes and the words. The illustrations capture the moments before a young child falls asleep and his/her "noticing" of each and every object around them. This sense of connection is a powerful precursor to language learning and the deepest sense of participation and belonging in the broader world.

Also among our stack of books that our grandchildren treasure is *The Magic Hat,* again by Mem Fox, which like Dr. Seuss,[49] has the ability to create more than a story and more than a dance. My wife reads *The Magic Hat* lyrically to children, and the figures move poetically with the antics of the Magic Hat. When she reads, "Ohhhhhhh…..the Magic Hat, the Magic Hat, it moves like this, it moves like that," every child becomes a character on the page, dancing and shouting the rhythms and rhyme of the story. This is not a passive story, but one that engages each child and instills energy to dance and have movement in every fiber of their body. Mem Fox understands that the read-aloud creates the momentum for the literacy experience and creates the momentum for a life of independent reading.

I've grown more appreciative of the powerful elixir of bonding that children bring to their adult providers when they spend time together. Our youngest grandchild is not yet two, but when we "road trip" together, and care for him each evening, our lives are enriched. Equally as important is the social drama playing out where

---

48 Margaret Wise Brown (1910-1952) American author of children's literature.

49 Theodor Seuss Geisel (1904-1991) Popular American author who wrote and illustrated 44 children's books.

the older siblings and cousins share life experiences with him. Our role is to provide a social context from which this young man will know love, kindness, and consideration for the world around him. We must, if we are to leave any substantial legacy, "teach the children well."

As we finally approached Onawa, I grew apprehensive that the cold weather of the last several days might diminish our opportunities to see wildlife and experience the natural world. In February it's hard to predict the conditions one might encounter. As we approached Blue Lake, we saw that the muskrat huts in the marsh were already attracting Canada geese for nesting sites. This area, opened up by the conditions of winter where much of the vegetation had died back or was buried in the snow, was larger then I remembered. I slowly lowered the window where my grandson was perched in his car seat. I spoke his name and pointing to the lake, "Look, geese!"

He replied, "geese!"

To our north, Blue Lake appeared frozen, the deep gray of the skyline did nothing to make the trip seem promising. We were only a few hundred yards into the park when I saw the familiar form of a muskrat feeding on the ice next to a muskrat hut. He looked like a sea urchin, with prickly shards of ice outlining his otherwise rounded form. When I mouthed the word, "muskrat," pointing as I spoke, Micah answered, "Papa, muskrat!" pointing to the muskrat just before it slid from the ice and disappeared beneath the water.

As we went deeper into the park I was amazed at the number of people walking near and around the lake. Near the north end of the lake, we took a turnoff to the north, where a turnabout lies close to a beaver hut. Here we met a trio of folks walking a beautiful Alaskan malamute. Micah is at a stage where he absolutely loves animals, particularly dogs. This one was gentle and calm and edged close to Micah. Micah was, at first, uncomfortable with the unknown, but quickly warmed up to the big dog. After fifteen minutes or so, as we prepared to leave, the dog whimpered, not wanting Micah to go.

As we were turning around, hordes of Canadas lifted off the lake into the sky. This created a grand commotion. "Micah," I said, "Look, Look!" We moved toward the middle of the park, stopping to experience the sounds of the geese traveling. Within every flock of geese there are bands whose vocalizations direct their behavior. Canadas are particularly vocal just before they lift into flight and as they lifted, Micah exhibited a great sense of anticipation, his face beaming, hands and arms gesturing, "look Papa, geese...geese...geese."

Several times I've been at the Desoto Wildlife Refuge in Missouri Valley, Iowa, to observe the hundreds of thousands of snow geese that arrive each fall, providing a clarity that one finds in nature.

As we neared the exit from the lake, we spied a small cabin in the woods. I spotted several deer close within the mix of trees and shrubs by the cabin. On closer examination, there was a small herd which became alarmed as we watched them. Departing with their white tails erect, bouncing stiffly as they ran, Micah watched intently and murmured, "puppies...puppies," I smiled knowing we were on the right track with identification, after all, puppies are mammals too.

Our road back home found us centered in a major migration of the Canada Geese. The sandhill cranes on the Platte River have a murmur of social gatherings as they commune on the prairie. This evening, though, belonged to the Canadas. As they staked out nesting sites, lifted from the water and ice, setting out to feed, Micah and I were deeply moved. He kept repeating, "geese, geese, geese..." For the next thirty miles or so, the sky was filled with bands of geese heading in all directions. At intervals, I would stop the car, get out, and hold Micah, bracing us as the geese swept majestically and loudly over us.

Yes *...there was a child went forth every day...* This child and I went forth daily after I picked him up at the daycare center. There is no greater love than what a child expresses when, after being taken to a daycare center, he is then picked up, assured that you would return. A ritual in our family is for the parent or grandparent to touch the child's heart and then take the child's hand and touch their heart in return. Micah would always come running, arms waving, out to greet me. Each day our road trip would take us to a nature center or to a park where we watched deer, wild turkeys and birds. In the child's eye, all animals are worthy and part of our "family."

Above a lone tree and an imposing windmill, geese soar high against a backdrop of an endless and breathtaking Midwestern sky.

Photo by Heather Bronkhorst

"Look Papa, geese. . . geese. . . geese."

Ode to a Coot

I'm sure,
there's a native artist
who when struck
with the notion
of painting waterfowl
after an hour of
contemplation
painted a coot.

One evening,
I sat on a hillside
overlooking a secluded bay
A cold October day
leaning toward dusk

Hundreds of coots
flowed with
the ebb of shivering blue
and purple waves
Whatever propelled
them it was both
efficient and obscure

They moved
as if choreographed
for loveliness
and precision
never out of place
equi-distance
each dancer
one from another.

As the light faded
the temperature dropped
accordingly

The darkened form
of the coots
silhouetted against
the silence.

Of Eiseley and Neihardt

Nebraska is a soulful place,
where the human spirit
refuses to be contained

Routing about
with the world
of essay and poems
Defining the elemental
fabric
of the land
its people
its sunsets
its work

Riding the rail
soulful fatigue
bone chilling
all absorbing cold

One
with the rain
the wind
the dust.

Harvest Time

It's harvest time
    Indian summer
        even as the morning sun
    brightens the day.

The small
    harvest moon glistens
        in the western sky
    as Jupiter fades.

Freshly harvested
    bean fields
    swept with golden
        chaff
    anoints the eye

Never are
    the contours
    more explicit

Corn stalks,
    brittle as
    they dry.

Deer find their
habitat shrinking
as every fiber within
quickens the pace

Red tail hawks
    join the harvest
tightening the bonds
of specie interdependence.

Road Trips With Papa

... But as humans we require support for our spirits, and this is what certain kinds of places provide. The catalyst that converts any physical location—any environment if you will—into a place, is the process of experiencing deeply.

—Alan Gussow[50]

Several years ago I found that Chloe, our then three-year-old granddaughter, and I had time on our hands. As I had recently retired, and Chloe needed some special care, we began reading her favorite books, making up songs, and even considered some tidying around the house. Though all of this was well and good for about two weeks, and still continues to be part of our routine, we knew we needed to devise a special time during the week for outdoor exploration. These times came to be known as "Road Trips with Papa."

We bought small backpacks for all our grandchildren, placing in them art supplies, journals, binoculars, and bird guides. In addition, I would always bring my camera. The road trips were not to be confused with a simple field trip, but an adventure that would require engagement, curiosity, and a passion for the

50 Alan Gussow (1931-1997) American artist and conservationist.

outdoors. In Chloe's mind, a Road Trip required time, patience, and a generous amount of good luck.

"Road Trips With Papa" came about from a personal reaction to conditions facing our own grandchildren. I feel we live in a deeply alienating society, where the freedom to explore, including inventive play in children, has been torn from their lives by a reverence for technology and a real concern for safety outside the home. I know full well that children need opportunities to feel a connection to places where they can grow in their understanding of stewardship and in return develop a very strong sense of belonging. Connection to a natural place allows children to learn about all aspects of habitat and wildness through observation and experience. Children learn from the very best expert, Mother Nature herself. As many have said, "Nature never lies."

Late one March morning, Chloe and I left Sioux City, Iowa, to go on a road trip to Ponca State Park in nearby Nebraska. Chloe's past recollections included a time when, "a snake ate that fat rat." On our way, we stopped at Martin's Airport in South Sioux City, Nebraska. Shortly after her birth Chloe was flown by helicopter, from St. Luke's Hospital in Sioux City to Children's Hospital in Omaha, Nebraska. Chloe knows the helicopter and its purpose well. As we approached Martin's, a medical helicopter flew over our heads. Chloe wanted to know if someone was sick or injured. Her personal sensitivities amaze me and have been heightened by our road trips as she connects to new surroundings and the environment.

As we approached the airport, Chloe asked that I stop the car. We lowered our windows to observe an American Robin (the first bird Chloe was ever able to identify). Overhead, one of the Air National Guard tankers swung low toward the Sioux City Airport. Chloe walked over to pose with the jet fighter exhibited at the entrance to the airfield. She also took great interest as a pilot readied his small one-engine plane—checking his controls, and idling the aircraft before taking off into a north wind.

As we left the airport, we noted the warming weather had melted the snow cover, even though the ground was frozen. Water, gathered in ditches and low indentations, accommodated a remarkable variety of migrating waterfowl. As we proceeded towards the park we couldn't help but notice Hooded Mergansers, Northern Shovelers, Mallards, and Coots in all the small ponds.

As we passed through Jackson, Nebraska, on the way to Ponca State Park, we were treated with a view of the first hawks of many we would spot perched on small trees, telephone poles, and posts. I asked Chloe, "How'd hawks perch before there were mile markers, fence posts, and telephone poles?" Just as we turned north toward Ponca, off Highway 20, a rough-legged hawk with a mole in its talons landed on a pole.

We pulled off to the side of the road, and Chloe watched attentively as the hawk shredded the mole, tearing off small strips. We found the hawks to be skittish on this day as the prairie offers little cover of protection.

Chloe was becoming somewhat of a fixture at Ponca State Park. As we entered through the heavy oak doors, the secretary motioned to her, "I'll bet you're here to see the snakes." As luck would have it, Chloe found her favorite snake, the rat snake staring intently at a black and white mouse. I pulled a chair over for her to use so she could study the snake. Chloe hunched over, her face in her hands as she watched the event that was about to happen.

The snake had recently lost its skin and glistened, his eyes fixed on the movements of the mouse only inches away. Chloe has no fear of snakes. She has held fox snakes and corn snakes since she was two. Over a year ago, Chloe began to watch this particular snake as it was fed. Her questions have increased in complexity and understanding over time. Her life's study is now being enhanced by the reality of this natural process.

She waited a bit, noting that the snake was inactive, and the mouse seemed very intent on eating small bits of seed found at the bottom of the case. "We'll come back when he is ready," she shared with me and moved on.

Chloe spent the first year of her life on a ventilator at Children's Hospital in Omaha. Sheltered, with loving folk by her side, music playing, and soft touches ever present, she developed a very keen sense of observation. She has, and always will have, congenital heart disease. That first year brought many surgeries to follow, resulting in Chloe having two titanium heart valves. Individuals who experience the loss of normal development often find that certain senses are heightened.

Chloe is insightful. She has seen and felt much in her young life, and the knowing of the assurances, with the ever presence of pain, give her a keen sensitivity to those around her.

Later, as we passed through the exhibit area in the center of the building, Chloe called my attention to a small turtle, a tern and a mounted red-tail hawk. She ran out of the room, anticipating her usual routine throughout, "her building." In an alcove on the east side of the building, children can play, observe, and note nature right outside the set of windows. In the fall and spring, turkeys, fox, squirrels, and various, indigenous wildlife scout the area for bits and pieces of sustenance. Chloe loves to look and watch the fish tanks nearby. She calls to the catfish by name. The fish, with his whiskers intact and inquisitive looks himself, allows Chloe to connect the dots—catbird, catfish, and cat—noting all similarities. She won't have to be taught how to apply what she has learned. In her mind, the world is a beautiful place filled with adventure and story. All children should know this type of classroom. Chloe waited a while, wanting to know if the catfish would say, "Meow."

We walked out the back door of the center and made our way past a small pond and bird feeders to an overlook facing eastward toward a portion of the Missouri River. This area will be forever wild and protected. Chloe listened to the call of the chickadee, stating, "Do you hear that Papa? The chickadee says, chick-a-dee-dee-dee, he says Miss DeeDee's name." Miss DeeDee was Chloe's kind and attentive preschool teacher. She couldn't wait to let Miss DeeDee know she had heard her name.

Because of the eco-tones (flood plains, the hills, and the prairie) interfacing at the Missouri River, Ponca State Park has, since its inception, been known as a great place for birding. In the brief period that we were there, we observed a red breasted nuthatch, a white breasted nuthatch, a dark eyed junco, several downy woodpeckers and others too numerous to mention.

Before returning inside, I spotted a junco which seemed to have just had an unfortunate encounter with a pane of glass. Chloe bent down, again resting on her little hands. "Papa," she spoke quietly, "is it a mommy bird or a daddy?"

"It's a daddy junco, Chloe." I mumbled.

"Papa," she spoke again. "Are there any babies nearby?"

As we continued our conversation, I noticed her reticence and concern. Chloe has such a need to know the boundaries of each species and to be assured that, "the babies," were comforted and safe. I know, as we continue our trips, that there will be times where death is inevitable, but for now I left it with, "No, Chloe, the babies are with their mom." Chloe would go on to share the story of the junco with family back home.

Near the entrance to the center, we heard one of the distinctive calls of the bright, red cardinal, "What cheer, what cheer, what cheer." At first, we had difficulty finding him. He was perched high in a tree on the east end of the parking lot. We moved cautiously toward him, taking pictures as we proceeded. The cardinal positioned himself to watch us. Otherwise, he seemed unconcerned. As we turned to walk back to the car, we imitated the cardinal's familiar phrase. We were delighted when he responded with the same. Chloe smiled, "Papa, he sounded our song."

Later that day, Chloe said to me, "Papa, aren't we lucky?"

"Why is that, Chloe?"

"We love the birds and the birds love us!" Our road trips have provided Chloe with a powerful relationship to all that nature has to offer and what Sylvan Runkel[51] called the "citizens of the natural world." Chloe has a unique, spiritual relationship in her connection to Ponca State Park. She is a member of that broader community, and truly a citizen of their world.

51 Sylvan T. Runkel (1906-1995) American naturalist, teacher, conservationist, pilot, musician, and co-author of wildflower guides.

Photo by Jeanette Hopkins

"Papa, aren't we lucky? We love the birds and the birds love us."

In a Child's Eye

In a child's eye,
    life is explored…
        critical questions
    apart from those
of adults.

Driving past
    the dead deer
        on the sideway of the road
    lies cold and still

    the traffic
        moves
    unabated—unconcerned.

To one small child
the deer is a friend
    lonely,
a mother.

The child asks,
    "Where are the baby deer?
        Is she cold?
            Can I touch her…
Is she dead?"

The Black Hills

After several days
in the Black Hills
of South Dakota,
I was enjoying
the abundance
of white tail deer,
butterflies and moths.

Yet,
there was a scarcity
of birds
notable in the exception
were the vultures
who rode the updrafts
and downdrafts…
avian bareback
riders.

The art of Nature
is in part
in her suddenness.
In this case,
glancing out
on a mountain stream
catching the form
of a belted kingfisher
fishing from a perch
on an electrical line.

In The Wild

Someone spoke
excitedly,
they'd found a snake.

There is something
about a snake
which refuses to be
ignored.
He was dark brown
and I was told,
a protected specie.

He flowed
across my hands…
leaning out into
space.
His dark eyes glistened;
he moved effortlessly
like mercury

He was as cool
as the out of doors
in mid October…
as succinct
as beauty
and truth.

Full Circle

The Woodshed

The woodshed on the far right takes its place with dignity and purpose, complementing the other New England farm buildings in their function and form.

The Woodshed

Indeed, the picturesque in human affairs and occupations is always born of love and humility, as it is in art or literature; and it quickly takes to itself wings and flies away at the advent of pride, or any selfish or unworthy motive.
—John Burroughs[52]

When I close my eyes and embrace my senses, I can still recall my familiarity with one small house. It was situated in a wooded area on the Ohayo Mountain along the road to Wittenberg, New York. On each end of the porch that ran the length of the front of the house was lattice work which, on the east end, supported a red climbing rose, the other end offered some privacy for a hammock which hung from the ceiling. On the corners of the porch were down spouts which descended from the eaves before emptying into neatly covered rain barrels. The proprietors of this humble estate were, in no particular order, the lime green snake who lived in the open lattice work near the hammock, a chipmunk who scurried about the stone work where he lived and stored nuts, a community of industrious eastern gray squirrels, a sundry of daddy long legs, and a short thin man, wearing a baseball cap with a leather bill. His pale blue eyes were framed by wire rimmed glasses.

52 John Burroughs (1837-1921) American naturalist.

His vest pocket held a mechanical pen, a six inch steel ruler, and a pencil. Most of the time he wore a dark green cotton shirt, neatly pressed, tucked in at the waist.

The first time I approached the house I was taken by its orderliness. Even before anyone opened the screen door to greet me, I felt comforted by the setting, the quietness, the gentle refrain of the wind in the pines. Crossing the porch, I took a glance through the front window with its many small frames of glass. My eyes were drawn to the form of his drafting table, on which was a line drawing of a barn with an open hayloft, and pulley. There was a Shaker-like simplicity to his lines—firm, fair, yet decisive.

He studied me as I stood silently, taking in the contents of his home. The living room was spartan by most standards, a modest cast iron stove, accompanied by sticks of kindling and several pieces of wood. A floor of wide pine boards, darkened from wear, pegged in place, setting a tone for the room, one of functionality and simplicity. The only floor covering was a large oval rag rug he had purchased from a neighbor. The side board was not imposing, fitting the dimensions and demeanor of the house. On a top shelf were two New England-style pewter candle holders.

Beside the stove was a Bentwood Adirondack rocking chair with a cushion held in place with two ties on the back. The seat was covered by an oval rug. Next to the chair was a square table roughly three feet by three feet in dimensions. It was covered by a plain white cotton cloth on which were placed a modicum of books and folded newspapers.

As we visited, he offered me a glass of water. We retired to the front porch where he explained why he had asked me to come. He started by saying, "I was visiting with your grandfather and I asked if he knew of someone who could work with me when I came up on the weekends from New York City." He then outlined some of the tasks he hoped to complete. The stone walls needed attention, freezing and thawing had dislodged some stones as had the busy hands of rabbit hunters and their hounds. He also wanted to plant Mountain Laurel, shrubs, and trees native to the Catskill Mountains. He wanted to build a woodshed with proper fittings. He wanted some help in learning to cut wood to fuel his bedroom fireplace and his stoves.

Interspersed in this conversation were questions about my interests and my plans after high school. We returned to his study. I noticed his dark green drafting pencils were organized in a cylindrical cardboard container, freshly sharpened, at the ready. Against the pencil holder were several strips of fine sandpaper and a three blade pen knife. Next to the pencils were two gum erasers, one with signs of recent use. Leaning against the drafting table were sheets of drawings in a manila folder. Later as I prepared to leave, he asked me if I liked to draw, and he then handed me several pencils of different hardness, a sharpener, and a plastic rectangle.

As we walked towards the gravel driveway, the rocks crunching beneath our feet, he talked about his life in New York City and of his weekly drive up the New York State Thruway. He said he could feel the stress of his work week lessening as he left the interstate and drove towards this mountain home.

Our first project grew in its complexity and purpose as we toiled. He wanted to build a woodshed, to be able to cut, stack, and handle his own wood. The woodshed we constructed was covered with hemlock boards, not planed, but rough hewn. The gaps between the boards were overlaid with three inch lathe. The door of the shed was built to mirror the door of the barn. As we worked and talked, we observed that every woodshed was a museum, not only because everything connected to the gathering and processing of wood was to be found there, but also because as we worked, many stories about the people who lived there would unfold, and their connections to their tools.

As the shed took form, so did the contents. Without exception, every saw had a fit and purpose. All were worn from use and their teeth sharpened before being put in place. We gathered the stories as we worked. The woodshed's contents hinted at the tanning industry which tanned pelts to be transformed into leather apparel from raccoon coats, to fine mink and fox coats and trimmings, resulting in the removal of many old growth hemlocks. Among the tools in the woodshed that loggers used were double-bitted axes and the one- and two-man saws. Logging was a major industry in the Catskills in the late 1800s until the mid twentieth century. The hemlock boards, used as siding, the slabs of wood cut into kindling, all were remnants from the saw mill at the Yankeetown Pond in Wittenberg. One of the stories shared in the woodshed was of a woodsman, of German heritage, who was noted for his gentle soul and brute strength. It involved a hemlock which when felled pinned a man between the butt end and the stump. Several men lifted on the log to no avail, until the woodsman grabbed onto the log and said, "Heave" and the log was lifted.

Axes of many dimensions were common, as was the necessity of harvesting a functional chopping block. We settled on a large block which we utilized to split wood. The chopping block was a section of hemlock, about three feet tall and of the same diameter. Wood was split using a single-bitted axe, raising the chunk of wood overhead with the axe before smashing it down on the block, using all the force one could muster. This process was continued until the wood was split. Once the season that supported splitting wood was over (late fall/early winter), the axe was left embedded in the stump.

At first, we split white pine without knots. Our endeavor involved splitting kindling into small thin pieces, to quick-start a fire. At one point, my new friend produced a hatchet in a sheath. I told him it might be useful to Boy Scouts working around a campfire, but was not very helpful in our work. We quickly graduated from splitting pine to knotty hard woods that tested our skills and patience. Anyone who has split wood by hand is familiar with the unforgiving knot which would grasp the axe head defying most efforts to extract it.

Soon we went about the business of cutting wood using a variety of saws. We started with the bow saw, cutting slabs and logs to length. As we worked we used rip saws with their shark like teeth to cut boards for the slab siding on the shed, cutting down the length of the boards. As we cut boards we used fine toothed cross cut saws. We progressed through the use of each of these axes and saws much as I had been taught by my grandfather and my father. Slowly but steadily my New York City friend was growing into a culture where the cutting of wood was a communal activity and where the two activities of sawing and splitting wood by hand was nearly an every day activity for months.

Later we built a cross buck frame and with a buck saw began the serious endeavor of filling the woodshed. The cross buck frame held the log snugly in place particularly helpful on pieces which had not tempered and dried. The frame allowed the cutter to brace against the log with a knee as it was sawed. As we worked we took turns sawing, retrieving and mounting logs to be cut. The woodpile was quickly mounting; we would soon be finished cutting and sorting.

Not all the wood that was cut was bound for the woodshed. Some of the wood was racked outside, buttressed between stout trees. Some of the wood needed to dry, some for more than one season.

The woodshed had a very special function, certainly, but also bordered on sanctity. Here the saws hung from pegs. Axes rested conveniently, freshly sharpened and wiped down with oil. Historically, the sharpening of some tools took place as men lit their pipes, leaned on a scythe, cycles, or axes, their wet stones in their back pockets and conversed. Although my friend from New York City did not smoke, many of the older outdoorsmen smoked pipes. They loaded their pipes using either a tin of tobacco or a folded pouch which had the advantage of enabling the smoker to load the pipe with a gentle dipping in the pouch, before tapping the tobacco into the pipe bowl. Pipe smokers had an appearance of being contemplative. This wasn't just an appearance though, when I stopped smoking, I continued to carry my empty pipe which I would engage with when thinking. The woodshed aged with each rainstorm, with each snow dusting, taking its place next to the small house, and barn, with dignity and purpose.

As my New York City friend picked up his mail at the Glenford Post Office, his circle of acquaintances grew as did the conversations he held. Folks often stopped to visit with him. In time, he joined the sportsmen's club and the fledgling fire department. In rural communities, at some time, everyone pitches in for its institutions to work.

In early fall, work surrounding the need for firewood picked up pace. Within a few weeks, deer season would open and many work activities would be set aside, including the processing of wood, for the duration of the season. Coinciding with Thanksgiving, the weather often grew decidedly colder, getting outside work completed became more compelling. Inside, the woodshed was nearly completed, so now the snow shovels were sharpened and polished and prepared for the onset of winter.

Now the woodshed was truly taking form. We began to fill the woodshed with cords of wood, ordered in rows, with larger chunks of wood serving as a base protecting the outer walls from the weight of the wood. As we proceeded, we would stop to marvel at what we had achieved as our projects began to come together. As we stacked wood, we were aware that we needed to have access to all sizes, species, and hardness of woods in order to stoke the stoves most efficiently. Segregated was a stack of small pieces whose sole purpose was to fuel the starting of a fire. Part of becoming acclimated to rural life was to recognize that each stick of wood, each nail, each nut, and each bolt was a resource that could make its need felt.

When it rained, we sat in the woodshed, listened to the sounds of the rain, the gentle refrain of water moving. We tidied about, tools were hung, planes were laid out high and dry, pencils placed in jars along with nails and screws. A pencil sharpener mounted.

No reflection had greater history than the steel jaw traps of varied sizes, some with identification tags dating back to when their owners were young and trapping was a survival skill, providing food, clothing and even income for some.

The woodshed was a cultured place, organized, a place of purpose and continuity, and shared at times with woodland species, brown bats, field mice, red squirrels, and opossums. The woodshed stood alongside the large vegetable gardens and various farm animals and fowl, which it properly addressed, affirming that money alone did not define the well being and standing of a family.

My grandfather's thoughtfulness in recommending me to his friend from New York City proved to be fortuitous, as he and I had worked together for years preparing gardens, planting shrubbery, and cutting and stacking wood for ourselves and for others. I was able to easily adapt to the transformative needs of my new friend as he became comfortable with life in the country. All of the activities involving axes, saws and tools had been taught to me by my grandfather, and by my father as well, connecting me not only to the life-sustaining process of working with my hands, but also of finding culture in the natural world as well as in human communities. We learn by doing.

Night Sky

It was late, too
late for many things.

Romance had wilted
before the frost;
His countenance deepened
with the perpetual stubble
of beard.

Still, he could not refrain
from looking wistfully
into the night sky
for the novocaine effect
of the Harvest Moon

Pencil drawing by Haley McClure

Dr. Bruce Hopkins is an educator, environmental writer, and historian. He brings to his work the soul of a naturalist and a passion for the positive welfare of children, older citizens, and anyone concerned with issues of social justice in the tradition of Thoreau and Emerson. His recent activities have included serving as a resident poet for pRhyme Time on the Prairie in Akron, Iowa, as well as at the The Sagamore Institute in Raquette Lake. New York. He works with high school seniors from Spencer, Iowa, at the Lakeside Lab in Spirit Lake, Iowa, each year. He was included in the "On the Fly" author project video series sponsored by UNESCO City of Literature in Iowa City, and Humanities Iowa. He has presented and read at numerous poetry and writing events throughout the Midwest and East Coast. Bruce's poetry has appeared in poetry journals throughout the United States. He is the author of a collection of essays and poetry, *When Foxes Wore Red Vests* (2010). A long-time resident of Iowa, he has also lived in New York and Nebraska.

Photo by Ken Horii

Howard N. Horii, FAIA, is an artist, architect and educator. He taught in the construction and facilities management department of Pratt Institute in New York for 44 years, practiced architecture with Grad Associates in New Jersey for 50 years and has been an artist all his life. The recipient of scholarships and awards from Redondo Beach High School in California, and from Cooper Union and Pratt in New York, Howard is an award-winning architect and a Fellow in the American Institute of Architects. He is past president of The New Jersey State Board of Architects, and served on the boards of The Newark, N.J. Community School of the Arts and the Newark, N.J. "ACE" (Architecture, Construction and Engineering) mentoring program for high school students. Howard and his wife Paula live in New Jersey and together have three children, Steve (Gail), Ken (Harriet) and Jane (Bob), and nine grandchildren, Mary, Bryan, Patrick, Kevin, Michael, John and Katherine Clancy, and Jina and Amelia Pappas-Horii.

The Ice Cube Press began publishing in 1993 to focus on how to live with the natural world and to better understand how people can best live together in the communities they share and inhabit. Using the literary arts to explore life and experiences in the heartland of the United States we have been recognized by a number of well-known writers including: Gary Snyder, Gene Logsdon, Wes Jackson, William Pitt Root, Patricia Hampl, Greg Brown, Jim Harrison, Annie Dillard, Ken Burns, Kathleen Norris, Janisse Ray, Craig Lesley, Alison Deming, Richard Rhodes, Michael Pollan, and Barry Lopez. We've published a number of well-known authors including: Mary Swander, Jim Heynen, Mary Pipher, Paul Engle, William Stafford, James Hearst, Bill Holm, Connie Mutel, John T. Price, Carol Bly, Marvin Bell, Debra Marquart, Ted Kooser, Stephanie Mills, Bill McKibben, and Paul Gruchow. We have won several publishing awards over the last twenty years. Check out our books at our web site, join our facebook group, follow us on twitter, visit booksellers, museum shops, or any place you can find good books and discover why we continue striving to, "hear the other side."

Ice Cube Press, LLC (est. 1993)
205 North Front Street
North Liberty, Iowa 52317-9302
steve@icecubepress.com
twitter @icecubepress
www.icecubepress.com

truth, truth, and more truth
stirred, swayed, mixed, and tumbled with
water, rivers, wind, and sun, alongside good intentions
for Laura Lee & Fenna Marie